GROWING into YOU!

GROWING into YOU!

An Inclusive, Shame-Busting, Get-Real Guide to Your Changing Body and Mind

Melissa Pintor Carnagey

QUIRK BOOKS
PHILADELPHIA

Text copyright © 2025 by Melissa Pintor Carnagey
Illustrations copyright © 2025 by Brianna Gilmartin

All rights reserved. Except as authorized under U.S. copyright law, no part of this book may be reproduced in any form without written permission from the publisher.

Library of Congress Cataloging-in-Publication Data
Names: Carnagey, Melissa Pintor, author. | Gilmartin, Brianna, illustrator.
Title: Growing into you! : an inclusive, shame-busting, get-real guide to your changing body and mind / Melissa Pintor Carnagey ; [illustrated by Brianna Gilmartin]
Description: Philadelphia : Quirk Books, [2025] | Includes bibliographical references and index. | Audience: Ages 10–14 | Summary: "An illustrated guide to puberty and changing bodies for tweens and young teens of all gender identities, including activities, conversation starters, and writing prompts"—Provided by publisher.
Identifiers: LCCN 2024043853 (print) | LCCN 2024043854 (ebook) | ISBN 9781683694311 (paperback) | ISBN 9781683694328 (ebook)
Subjects: LCSH: Puberty—Juvenile literature. | Sexual health—Juvenile literature. | Gender identity—Juvenile literature. | Sex instruction for children. | Sex instruction for teenagers.
Classification: LCC QP84.4 .C37 2025 (print) | LCC QP84.4 (ebook) | DDC 613.9071—dc23/eng/20241112
LC record available at https://lccn.loc.gov/2024043853
LC ebook record available at https://lccn.loc.gov/2024043854

ISBN: 978-1-68369-431-1

Printed in China

Typeset in DM Sans, Edmondsans, FreightText Pro, Gingerstraw, and Sketchnote Square

Designed by Paige Graff
Cover and interior illustrations by Brianna Gilmartin, except for stock illustrations by DiCreate on pages 16–17, 26–27, 78–79, and 128–129

Quirk Books
215 Church Street
Philadelphia, PA 19106
quirkbooks.com

10 9 8 7 6 5 4 3 2 1

For Tyson, Owen, and all the tweens and young teens who deserve to feel prepared and supported during puberty

Contents

Introduction

About the Reader (That's You!)   9

About the Author (That's Me!)   12

Part 1: What's the Deal with Puberty, Anyway?

Puberty Is . . .   18

Puberty Is Not . . .   20

Part 2: How Does Your Body Change During Puberty?

Puberty Starts Here!   28

All Things Anatomy: What's Up Down There?   37

Signs of Puberty   54

Puberty Across the Gender Universe   65

Part 3: How Do I Take Care of My Body During Puberty?

About Body Image	80
Hygiene Hacks	87
Period Power!	95
Planning for Self-Care	122

Part 4: How Can I Connect with Myself and Others During Puberty?

Exploring Pleasure	130
Practicing Consent and Boundaries	135
Being a Good Friend During Puberty	142
More Than Friends?	147

The End . . . or Just the Beginning?	150
Trusted Resources to Continue the Learning	153
Glossary of Terms	156
References	164
Index	167
Acknowledgments	173

Introduction

Did you know that breast buds aren't something just girls develop?

Or that voice changes don't happen just to boys?

What about the fact that once a person has their first period, it can take up to five years for their cycle to become regular?

What if I told you that all these facts have one thing in common:

If you're reading this, you might be looking for more information about what puberty means for your body, your brain, and your emotions. Or maybe a trusted adult gave you this book to read, and you're not sure what you'll get out of it yet. Here's what I can promise: in this guide, you'll find lots of information about topics such as bodies, puberty, gender identity, consent, and healthy relationships.

In my experience, talking or even thinking about these topics might make you feel one or more of the following ways:

Whatever you are feeling is totally welcome here. The only feeling we don't want to invite to this party is shame, because shame can make you think there's something wrong or bad about you, your curiosities, your body, or your puberty journey. Nothing is further from the truth!

ABOUT THE READER (THAT'S YOU!)

This book is for you because you deserve to know what to expect during puberty—and you deserve to learn about it in an inclusive way, using language that aligns with your identity. This book is also helpful for parents, caregivers, and trusted adults who may not have had this kind of honest, shame-free education growing up, and who want to learn ways to support their young person during puberty.

You know yourself best.
You are unique, unlike anyone else on Earth.*

*Yes, even if you are a twin!

Who Are You Today?

Throughout our lives, and especially during puberty, we experience many changes: in our bodies, in how we think and feel, and in how we relate to others and the world around us. Take a moment to think about who you are right now. Let's capture and honor this version of you by answering these questions in a notebook.

* How old are you?
* Which pronouns do you use? (Pronouns are words like *she*, *he*, *they*, and *ze*, which people use when they're referring to us but not using our name.)
* What three words would you use to describe yourself today?
* What do you feel happiest doing?
* What's your favorite snack? (Feel free to munch on it while you read!)

In your notebook, draw a picture of yourself that includes the unique things that make you *you*! Include ways you like to express yourself. Maybe it's through your hairstyle or the clothes you wear. You can also draw a background that shows you in your favorite place or enjoying your favorite things. There's no wrong way to draw yourself!

This is the *you* today.

You will continue to grow and change.
Who will you be in the future?
You get to decide!

ABOUT THE AUTHOR (THAT'S ME!)

You might be curious about who's written this book. Hi, I'm Melissa. I use she/her/hers or they/them/theirs pronouns.

I'm a nonbinary sexual health educator and social worker who teaches young people and families about topics like bodies and puberty. I created an online platform called Sex Positive Families because I'm passionate about helping young people, parents, and caring adults learn how to talk more comfortably about these very human things. I've taught interactive workshops about bodies and puberty for thousands of tweens, teens, and parents from around the world, and I've even included some of their thoughts within sections of this book. If you're curious about these workshops, visit giypuberty.com to learn more and sign up. We'd love to have your family join us!

─── TELL ME MORE! ───

What does sex positive mean? The answer might surprise you! It simply means having an open, shame-free understanding of bodies, sexuality, and sex.

Being a sex-positive family means that honest conversations and education about these topics are treated as a healthy part of growing up, not avoided or silenced. Research shows that when young people receive sexual health education and support from their trusted adults, they are better able to make informed decisions about their bodies, relationships, and sex, and know who to turn to for guidance when they need it. Puberty education is one of the many stepping stones to building a solid foundation of health: physical health, sexual health, and mental health.

When I was a tween and teen, talking about bodies, puberty, and sexual health was taboo. It was hard to get accurate information or feel comfortable talking to my parents, which left me feeling alone, confused, and unsure when the many changes began to happen to me. I wish I had a trusted adult who made it comfortable for me to open up. I've learned that my experience is not so uncommon, and that many grown-ups did not have enough support like I did—but they want a better experience for their own children.

Now that I'm a parent of three young people, I've been able to break this cycle and have countless conversations and teachable moments with my kids to help them navigate their own puberty journeys without shame or taboo.

If I could time-travel to my tween years, I'd give this book to myself and my parents. I believe if we'd had resources like this to normalize conversations about puberty, our family may have felt more comfortable connecting, and it could have helped me to feel better prepared, informed, and supported through my puberty journey.

HOW TO GET STARTED

Throughout the book, you'll find journal prompts (Let's Write About It!) and activity ideas (Let's Have Fun with It!). I recommend keeping a pen and a notebook or piece of paper nearby while reading so you can write down your responses, thoughts, and questions. You can keep them to yourself, but I also encourage you to share any questions and feelings that come up with your trusted adults, if you feel safe to do so. You might feel weird at first if you aren't used to talking about these subjects with them, and it might not go "perfectly" the first few times you try—but don't let shame join the conversation. To help you connect with trusted adults on these puberty topics, you'll notice that each section of this book also includes a Let's Talk About It! section with conversation starters. Talking openly is the best way to learn from one another!

Who counts as a trusted adult? Trusted adults can be found in many different roles and parts of your life. They could be a parent, stepparent, older sibling, aunt, uncle, grandparent, godparent, older cousin, teacher, counselor, youth leader, coach, pastor, mentor, nanny, neighbor, or other member of your community. They could also be a professional provider you go to for services like therapy or medical care.

However, their title or the role they play in your life doesn't guarantee that you'll see this person as someone safe and trustworthy to turn to when you have questions or need support during puberty. You get to determine who is a trusted adult in your life.

To help you identify a trusted adult in your world, think about someone who has some of these traits:

- Easy to talk to
- Kind
- Makes time for you
- A good listener
- Patient
- Respectful
- Honest
- Trustworthy
- Reliable
- Affirms and respects your identities
- Nonjudgmental
- Respects your boundaries
- Feels safe to you (this is a big one!)

Which qualities feel most important to you when you are looking for support? Are there other qualities you would add to this list? As you navigate changes to your body and mind during these years, you can refer to this list when you encounter new people and situations.

It's also possible that a trusted adult is not available to you right now, or that you may prefer to keep the things you're learning to yourself. That's okay, too. Use this book and its resources in whatever ways feel most comfortable to you.

Finally, I invite you to use this book at your pace—because puberty is a journey, not a race. You might skim some of the chapters, try out some of the conversation starters or activities, skip around, or go through the entire book from start to finish. Some of the information may not apply to you yet, but you can revisit it when you're ready. Some of the information may never apply to you, but I encourage you to read those sections, too. Learning about bodies, identities, and puberty experiences that are different from your own is an important way to foster empathy for and appreciation of others. You'll notice this book was written inclusively to help you and other tweens and young teens of many different bodies, gender identities, and puberty journeys see yourselves reflected and learn many different facts about growing up.

No matter how you experience this book, I hope it becomes a useful guide to support you along the journey of **growing into you!**

> "It's not just hairy armpits!"
>
> —Lucas, 11 years old

PART 1

What's the Deal with Puberty, Anyway?

Puberty Is . . .

You probably already know a bit about puberty—from school, in pop culture, by seeing other people go through it, or because you're experiencing puberty right now! When you hear the word *puberty*, what words come to mind?

Take a moment to explore this word cloud, based on one made by real tweens and their trusted adults in one of the Growing Into You!™ virtual puberty workshops.

If any of these words are new to you, that's okay! As you can see, there are a range of physical, emotional, social, and mental changes that happen during puberty—and we'll learn about all of them.

— TRY THIS —

* Point to the words in the cloud that relate to emotions during puberty.
* Find the words that relate to body parts and physical changes during puberty.
* What words would you add to the cloud?

Now let's look at a definition of puberty:

Puberty is a process of changes that cause a child's body to mature into an adult body.

This maturing develops the brain, bones, emotions, and even the ability to reproduce. But, wait, you might be wondering—what does it mean to reproduce? *How do people reproduce?* Keep reading; I'll give you all the info later in this book! (Or if you're like me and don't like waiting, you can hop over to page 43 for more info about this!)

Puberty Is Not . . .

1. **A race. Your body has its own pace!** Did you know that every person goes through their own unique puberty experience in their own timing? Not even identical twins go through the exact same changes at the exact same time. There are as many unique puberty experiences as there are people on Earth!

2. **Something that happens overnight, or over a summer.** Puberty happens in stages that can take five to 10 years to be completed. For many people, these changes begin between ages 8 and 10 and end between ages 18 and 21. For transgender young people who use puberty blockers during adolescence, it's possible to experience changes later in adulthood, like having a second puberty once they are no longer taking puberty blockers. (We'll learn more about puberty blockers on page 72.) Either way, puberty doesn't happen overnight; it happens bit by bit over several years. This means you'll have some time to get to know your body as it is changing.

Growing into You!

3. **Binary.** The word *binary* refers to something that has just two elements. Puberty is not binary because it is not limited to only two types of experiences based on gender or body parts—for example, "girl puberty" or "boy puberty." Each person's body and identities are diverse and unique. The changes you will go through depend on the particular body parts you have and how they function. We'll learn more about this in "All Things Anatomy" starting on page 37, so you can better understand what to expect in your unique puberty journey.

Real Questions, Real Answers

Asking questions is how we learn. Throughout this book, I'll share answers to some of the questions I've received from tweens who attend the Growing Into You!™ virtual puberty workshops. Maybe you've wondered about some of these things, too!

Do dogs and cats go through puberty?

Yes! Animals also go through growth that causes physical and behavioral changes, brought on in stages by hormones that support reproduction. The process and timing can look different for every type of animal. Dogs typically experience puberty between six months and two years old, which is when puppies transform into adult dogs. Dogs with a uterus experience discharge, bleeding, and heat cycles (called estrus), which make it possible for them to reproduce. Dogs with testicles experience the descending of these parts into their scrotum during puberty, similar to what happens to humans with testicles. Cats experience puberty in similar ways and timing. Because humans have complex brains, we experience social changes during puberty, too—like having crushes, changing friendships, and evolving identities—that are quite unique from the experiences of the rest of the animal kingdom.

My mom told me that she started growing boobs and had her period at age 10. Will puberty happen just like this for me, too?

Sometimes genetics—the traits you can inherit from your parents and ancestors—can cause similarities in puberty experiences, but most of the time your changes and when they happen will be completely unique from your relatives' experiences.

Some of my friends are getting taller, and their voices are getting deeper. I haven't experienced this yet! Am I a late bloomer?

It's common to wonder if your body is doing what it should when you think it should. And you might be tempted to compare yourself to your friends or to other people around you. You might even hear other people compare your body to those of others or use terms like "late bloomer," as if puberty is a competition! Talking this way about puberty and bodies is not helpful or accurate and can contribute to feelings of insecurity. Try to remember:

==Puberty is not a race. My body has its own pace.==

If you're worried or wondering about how your body is changing, talk with a trusted adult. This can be a good opportunity to visit with your pediatrician or another medical provider who can help you understand your unique puberty journey and answer your questions.

Let's Write About It!

This section is just for your thoughts! Grab your notebook, paper, or device, and remember, there are no wrong answers.

* Think of other things that go through physical changes, like plants, animals, or seasons. Draw a few of them in their different forms—before, during, and after their changes.
* Now think about yourself just two years ago. Make a list of some ways you've changed since then. For example, have you experienced physical changes like getting taller, growing breasts, or a change in hairstyle? How about social changes, like making new friends or trying new hobbies?
* Celebrate your uniqueness! Think of three things that make you totally one of a kind. Jot them down.

Let's Talk About It!

With a parent, trusted adult, or friend, read these questions out loud and start chatting together.

* Sometimes puberty can feel awkward to talk about. Why do you think that is?
* To ask a trusted adult: How old were you when you started going through puberty? Who taught you about puberty or helped you through it? If you did not have support, how did that feel?

Let's Have Fun with It!

Take the learning into your world by trying out this activity.

Create an Affirmation Station to help remind you of how unique and amazing you are, *exactly* as you are! Affirmations are positive, motivational statements that can improve your confidence and self-esteem. These phrases may feel true for you, or they can represent a feeling you *want* to feel true for you. Some examples of affirmation statements are:

I believe in myself.
I am brave.
I am enough, just as I am.
I can do hard things.

* Jot down three or more affirmations using sticky notes or create them digitally to print out or save on your device. You can make up your own affirmations or use the above examples. Put them somewhere you can easily and regularly read them to yourself, like on your bathroom mirror, next to your bed, in your locker, or as digital wallpaper.
* Stand in front of a mirror, look yourself in the eye, and say your affirmations out loud. Try this at least once a day, in the morning or before bed. It's totally okay if it feels awkward or silly the first few times. Keep practicing until it feels more comfortable.

"Puberty is a whole mood!"

—Thea, 13 years old

PART 2

How Does Your Body Change During Puberty?

Puberty Starts Here!

Now that we know some of the basics about puberty, let's talk about what makes those changes begin in the first place.

Puberty starts within the brain, through two parts that work together. These two parts are called the hypothalamus and the pituitary gland. When people begin puberty, the hypothalamus tells the pituitary gland to release hormones.

—— **FUN FACT** ——

Hormones are chemicals that act like messengers, carrying signals for the body to begin changing and to start other processes in the body. For more, see "Getting to Know Your Hormones" on page 30.

Three hormones that trigger the start of puberty are called estrogen, progesterone, and testosterone. These hormones are typically found in all bodies and are mainly produced in body parts like the testes and the ovaries. People who were assigned female at birth or who have ovaries typically produce higher levels of estrogen and progesterone in their bodies. People who were assigned male at birth or who have testes typically produce higher levels of testosterone in their bodies.

When a tween has higher estrogen and progesterone levels in their body, certain puberty experiences are more likely to happen, such as:

* growing breasts
* having a period
* widening of the hips and pelvic area

When a tween has higher testosterone levels in their body, other puberty experiences are more likely to happen to them, such as:

* developing facial hair
* deepening of the voice
* increased muscle growth

── TELL ME MORE! ──

Many of us were assigned both a sex and gender, at birth or even earlier, by our parents or medical professionals who helped birth us. These identity labels are often used interchangeably, but they actually mean different things.

Sex assigned at birth, also called "biological sex," is a label that is given to a baby when they are born, such as *female*, *male*, or *intersex*. The label is usually based on an assessment of their external genitals. For example, a baby is assigned female when they have a vulva and clitoris. A baby is assigned male when they have a penis and scrotum. A baby might be assigned intersex if they have a noticeable variation to their genitals that isn't considered typically female or typically male.

Gender is an aspect of a person's identity that is influenced by how they express themselves in connection to society's norms, expectations, and stereotypes of masculinity and femininity. Some of the many examples of gender identities are boy/man, girl/woman, transgender, nonbinary, agender, and genderqueer. A person's gender identity can't truly be determined by another person, or by physical characteristics; only you know who you are and how you wish to express yourself. Gender identity can develop over time, throughout a person's life, and isn't always a fixed label.

> The truth is that sex and gender assignments were created by people over time to reinforce the myth that bodies and identities exist in a binary of only two distinct, opposite, and disconnected forms. Bodies and identities are much more diverse and can have many variations. Knowing this can help you respect and celebrate others as they are and encourage you to embrace your most authentic self without being limited by society's expectations.

GETTING TO KNOW YOUR HORMONES

Hormones, and other naturally occurring chemical messengers in the body called neurotransmitters, play a role in regulating mood—not just during puberty, but throughout our entire lives. These chemical messengers can be impacted by everyday things like the foods we eat, how hydrated we are, the amount of stress we experience, how much sleep we get, and how much physical activity we do.

When our hormones and neurotransmitters are triggered, they cause us to experience different emotions, such as happiness, sadness, excitement, stress, irritability, and anger. Some that are responsible for these mood changes are called serotonin, dopamine, cortisol, oxytocin, and endorphins.

* **Serotonin** is made by nerve cells within the body. Serotonin helps regulate our sleep and moods and plays a big part in healing wounds.

* **Dopamine** is made within the brain and the adrenal glands, which are located on the top of the kidneys. Dopamine helps regulate our movements, memory, moods, sleep, motivation, and ability to feel pleasure. (Learn more about pleasure on page 130.)

* **Cortisol** is made and released by the adrenal glands. Cortisol affects every organ and tissue in our bodies, regulating the stress response, metabolism, the immune system, blood pressure, and sleep patterns.
* **Oxytocin** is made by the hypothalamus and is released into the bloodstream by the pituitary gland. Oxytocin plays a big role in many human and social behaviors like feeling trust, bonding, and forming romantic attachment to others. It also causes the contractions needed during childbirth, breastfeeding, and ejaculation.

* **Endorphins**, like oxytocin, are also made by the hypothalamus and released into the bloodstream by the pituitary gland. Endorphins help relieve pain, reduce stress, and regulate mood. They can be released during activities like running, dancing, swimming, eating, and sex. (Learn more about sex on page 50.)

> ——— **FUN FACT** ———
>
> Hormones are with us our whole lives and continue to trigger changes in later life stages. For people with ovaries and/or higher estrogen levels, the stages are called *perimenopause* and *menopause*. For people with testes and/or higher testosterone levels, the stage is called *andropause*. Parents, grandparents, or other older adults in your life likely know a thing or two about these stages!

Knowing how our bodies work helps us to better understand the signals our body sends each day—and when we pay attention to these signals, we can make decisions that help us feel well and balanced.

Real Questions, Real Answers

Are mood swings just a "girl" thing?

Since hormones are responsible for mood shifts, and we *all* have different hormones in our bodies, it is a myth that only one gender experiences mood swings. The idea that mood swings are something only girls experience is an example of a **stereotype** and is a result of **misogyny**. A stereotype is a mistaken belief about a particular group of people, which can lead to harmful or limiting assumptions about all people of that group. Misogyny is hatred, prejudice, or discrimination against women or girls and is rooted in the belief that women or girls are inferior to men or boys.

Boys and men also experience big shifts in their moods, but social pressures can impact how these feelings are expressed. **Toxic masculinity** is a harmful perception of manliness that discourages boys and men from expressing feelings like sadness, disappointment, and fear—but often encourages them to express anger as a way of asserting power. For example, a boy who expresses sadness or cries might be mocked or told to "man up." On the other hand, he might be encouraged to channel his uncomfortable feelings into physical aggression or harsh words.

Stereotypes, misogyny, and toxic masculinity are all harmful influences that limit us. Being aware of these constructs can help us recognize when they show up in our everyday lives, and make choices to resist them. No matter your gender, feeling the full spectrum of emotions, and learning healthy ways to manage them, are important parts of being human—through puberty and beyond.

My moods have been feeling more unpredictable and harder to control lately. Is that because of puberty?

It's very common to experience shifts in your mood during puberty. Sometimes these shifts happen because of hormones, sometimes they are due to outside events, and sometimes the reason isn't clear. Your body is going through lots of changes. Try to be kind to yourself and notice patterns: Is there a time of day you usually feel best, or a time during the week? Do you tend to feel worse or better after a certain activity? Our moods are often great teachers, letting us know when we might need more rest, a snack, some movement, a conversation with a friend, or time alone. Check out the conversation starters and journal prompts on page 35 for helpful ways to further explore changes in your mood.

If your mood ever feels down or sad for longer periods of time, if you're no longer enjoying activities you used to, or if you're having trouble sleeping, eating, or focusing, talk with a trusted adult. These could be signs of depression or other diagnoses that a mental health professional can assist you in managing. Sometimes counseling or even medication can be helpful. Either way, know that you are not alone, and you deserve to have support and care.

Let's Write About It!

This section is just for your thoughts! Grab your notebook, paper, or device, and remember, there are no wrong answers.

* Pick one of the following emotions and write about the last time you felt it: angry, disappointed, frustrated, overwhelmed, sad.
* Now pick one of the following emotions and write about the last time you felt it: excited, proud, loved, surprised, motivated.
* Write a list of ways you could take care of yourself when you're experiencing big emotions. For example, could you take deep breaths, listen to music, talk with someone you trust, read, take a walk, draw, play a video game or sport, or something else?

Let's Talk About It!

With a parent, trusted adult, or friend, read these questions out loud and start chatting together.

* When you're feeling big emotions, how do you like to be treated by others at home? For example, do you like to have some time by yourself, or prefer to have someone to talk to? Do you like a hug? Something else? Consider sharing your answers with the people you live with, and asking them about their own preferences.
* To ask a trusted adult: As a kid, how comfortable did you feel expressing your feelings to your family? What about with your friends? How do you think this has shaped the way you process emotions today?

Let's Have Fun with It!

Take the learning into your world by trying out this activity.

While watching a show, movie, or YouTube video that involves people or characters interacting, mute the sound and remove any captions. Observe the facial expressions and body language of the people in each scene and then guess what emotion you think each person is experiencing.

Are they happy, excited, scared, sad, angry, frustrated, lonely, embarrassed, or another feeling? How can you tell?

You can do this activity on your own, or invite a friend, parent, or trusted adult to try it with you. Consider or discuss the following questions:

* When was the last time you felt that emotion?
* What was going on?
* What did that emotion feel like in your body?
* If it felt like a difficult emotion, what did you need to help you through that feeling?
* When you notice someone experiencing that emotion, what can you do to support them?

All Things Anatomy: What's Up Down There?

Your body will likely change quite a bit during your tween and teen years, which can prompt all kinds of feelings: anxiety, excitement, curiosity, and more. Whatever you're feeling is normal and okay. In this section, we'll talk about body parts on both the outside and inside of the genital and pelvic regions of the body, including the vulva, vagina, uterus, penis, scrotum, and testicles.

Learning the anatomical terms for body parts and how they function can help us feel empowered and prepared. It's important to call things what they are, without shame or taboo—and knowing the accurate terms helps you speak more confidently about your body if you need support for any reason. I also include slang terms or euphemisms that you might hear people using in place of anatomical words. You might have other words you prefer to call your own body parts. That's totally cool and can feel empowering, too!

There are lots of illustrations in this book to give you an idea of what these body parts can look like, but remember what we've learned so far: bodies are unique, and there are many different ways that bodies can form and change over time, so these pictures are not necessarily representative of what every single body looks like. It's also totally okay if reading these terms or seeing the illustrations causes some discomfort or makes you giggle; this can be part of your learning and growing, too! Just keep in mind that there's nothing bad or shameful about bodies.

VULVA, VAGINA, UTERUS, AND MORE!

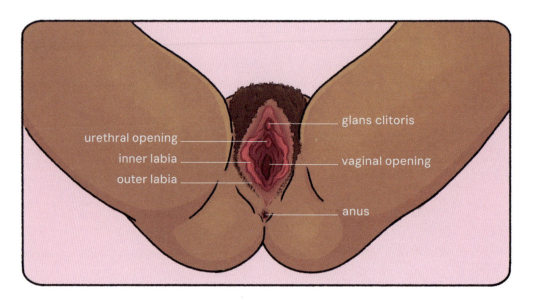

Let's start with the vulva, which is the outside area that surrounds the vaginal opening. People sometimes refer to the vulva as the vagina, but the vagina is actually on the inside, which we'll learn more about below.

The vulva includes a few different parts such as the labia and clitoris. Labia are folds of skin that can exist in different sizes, shapes, and skin tones. The labia consist of the outer labia (also called the labia majora) and the inner labia (also called the labia minora).

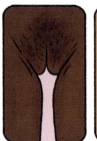   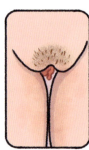 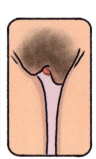

The outer labia commonly grow pubic hair during puberty. Some people choose to trim or remove this hair. Some people choose to leave it be. What a person decides to do with the hair that grows on their body, and especially on their genitals, should always be their choice. If you ever want to change the way your body hair looks, talk with a trusted adult to make sure you have the right tools and access to a safe method. (Learn more about body hair on pages 55 and 89.)

The labia's job is to protect the openings to the inside of the vulva. There are two: the urethral opening and the vaginal opening. The **urethral opening** is connected to the **urethra**, which is a tube inside the body that connects to the bladder. The **bladder** is an organ where urine (or pee) develops. Urine comes out through the urethral opening. It's important to note that people do not pee out of the vagina; the vagina has a completely separate hole called the vaginal opening. More on that body part soon!

Then there is the **clitoris** or clit for short. The glans clitoris, or external tip of the clitoris, is made of erectile tissue, which means it can become erect or firm up. It is very sensitive because it has thousands of nerve endings. If you have this body part, you may have noticed that it feels good if you are cleaning that area or when it rubs up against your clothing, or if you touch it through masturbation. *Masturbation* means to touch your own body for pleasure. (Learn more about this on page 95.) Stimulating the clitoris can cause a tickling or tingling feeling, which can lead to the vestibular bulbs filling with blood and then releasing after a series of contractions called an orgasm. This can also cause ejaculation, which is the release of clearish, whitish fluid from the vagina. There's nothing weird, bad, or wrong about this. The vagina is just doing its job!

The fact that the glans clitoris and the penis are both made up of erectile tissue with thousands of nerve endings makes them homologous (pronounced huh-MAH-luh-guhs), which means they are separate body parts with similar features.

The rest of the clitoris lives inside the body and looks like this:

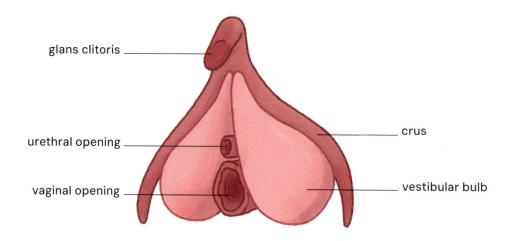

> ──── **FUN FACT** ────
>
> The clitoris grows in size throughout a person's life, not just during puberty. The full body of the clitoris, from the tip of the glans to the end of the crus, can grow to as long as five inches.

A third hole is the **anus.** You might call it a butthole. This is where gas (also known as farts) and feces (or poop) exit the body. The anus connects to the intestine, colon, and stomach, which all are responsible for breaking down the food we eat. During puberty, pubic hair often grows around the anus.

Now let's talk about some of the body parts that are on the inside of the pelvic area, starting with the vagina. The **vagina** has a muscular tube shape that is typically around three to five inches long. It can expand or retract, depending on the body's needs. The most common reason for the vagina to expand in size is childbirth, when the vagina expands to make room for a baby to pass through. The vagina retracts in the days and weeks following the birth and returns to its original size.

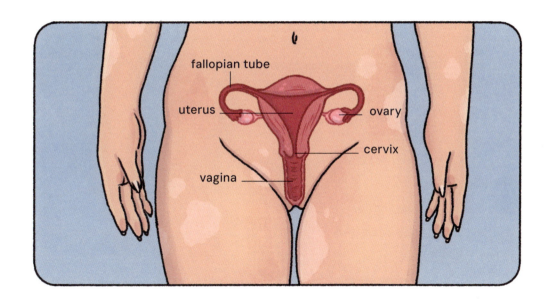

—— FUN FACT ——

Did you know there are only two ways for babies to be born? One way is by passing through the vagina, and the other way is via a cesarean section, or C-section. A C-section is a surgical procedure where a medical professional makes an incision wide enough and deep enough in the abdomen of the pregnant person so they can reach inside the uterus and remove the baby. Do you know which way you were born?

The vagina creates fluids called cervical mucus and vaginal discharge. Vaginal fluids are naturally acidic, so they can bleach or lighten the color of dark underwear. This doesn't mean the body is dirty, or that the underwear is ruined. It means a powerful body is doing its job! People with vaginas can also experience **nocturnal emission**, or wet dreams, during which vaginal fluids leave the body while a person is sleeping. This is totally normal.

Throughout each month, the vagina makes natural secretions to regulate and clean itself. Since it has these self-cleaning abilities, a person with a vagina should not try to insert anything inside to clean it. We'll talk more about genital hygiene in the "Hygiene Hacks" section on page 87.

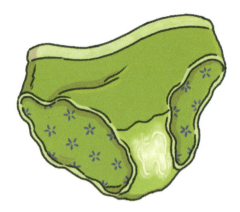

The vagina leads to the cervix, which kind of looks like a donut with a small opening in the middle. The cervix is another body part that can expand or retract and typically expands only when needed during childbirth, so a baby can pass through the opening. You can think of the cervix as a protective doorway keeping certain things from entering the uterus, such as tampons, period products, or water when you're bathing or swimming.

The uterus is the organ where a developing baby, or fetus, grows. This means that we all started out in a uterus; it was our first home! When there isn't a developing fetus inside, the uterus is about the size of a pear. When there is a fetus, the uterus expands as the fetus grows.

The uterine lining (also called endometrium) is made up of connective tissue that develops throughout the month with the help of hormones like estrogen. If a person is pregnant, that uterine lining remains and helps support the baby's needs while it grows. If there's no baby growing, the uterine lining sheds and exits the body through the vagina. This process is called menstruation (or a period), and it typically starts to happen during puberty. A person that has periods might experience some cramping within the first day or so of menstruation, when the uterus is contracting to loosen that uterine lining. We'll discuss more about menstruation on page 95.

On each side of the uterus is a fallopian tube with an ovary attached at its end. Fallopian tubes are slender passageways. Ovaries are oval-shaped glands about the size of an almond. Each ovary contains hundreds of thousands of eggs. These eggs are called ova, or ovum if you're talking about just one. People with ovaries are typically born with these eggs in their ovaries.

> **—— FUN FACT ——**
>
> Ova are around one-tenth the size of a pencil dot. This sounds small, but they are actually the largest cell in the human body!

During the menstrual cycle, at least one ovum will leave an ovary. This process, called ovulation, usually takes a few days. The ovum travels down the fallopian tube and chills out there for a few days, in case a sperm (which is short for spermatozoon) shows up.

How does a sperm get there? This can happen through sex, or it can happen through assisted reproduction, which uses one of many methods for bringing sperm and an ovum together.

> **—— TELL ME MORE! ——**
>
> Two of the most common assisted reproduction methods are called **in vitro fertilization (IVF)** and **intrauterine insemination (IUI)**. These methods, typically done with the help of a fertility doctor, can enable people to become parents when conceiving through sexual intercourse is not an option.

If no sperm shows up to join the egg, that egg continues to travel down to the uterus, where it dissolves. The developing uterine lining—made up of blood, mucus, and connective tissue—sheds and exits the vagina since there is no fetus to use it. It typically takes about three to seven days for all of the uterine lining and menstrual fluids to exit, and this is what we call a period. You'll learn more about period care, and self-care during a period, on page 95.

PENIS, SCROTUM, TESTICLES, AND MORE!

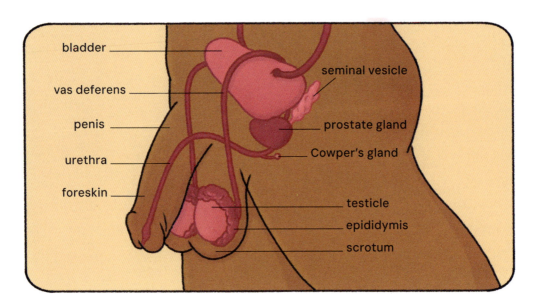

The penis is an organ on the outside of the body. It is unique to every individual in its size, shape, and skin tone. During puberty, pubic hair typically begins to grow around the base of the penis, while the shaft of the penis usually does not grow pubic hair. Just like the glans of the clitoris, the penis is made of erectile tissue that can feel sensitive to the touch. When a penis experiences an erection, blood flows into the penis, which causes it to firm up and become hard. You might hear this referred to as a boner, but there actually aren't any bones in the penis!

Erections can be quite common during puberty and should not be made fun of or used to shame someone. They can happen when a person is either awake or asleep, while thinking of something that feels really pleasing to them, or if the penis is stimulated. Waking up with an erection is often called having "morning wood." Sometimes, especially during puberty, the penis can also ejaculate (release semen) while a person is sleeping. If you have a penis and you notice a whitish, sticky fluid in your underwear when you wake up, this is the result of nocturnal emission (or wet dreams), and it is totally normal.

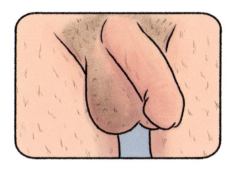 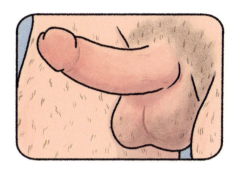

This is an example of a penis when it is not erect, or flaccid.

This is what it can look like when it becomes erect.

At birth, a penis typically has an outer skin that extends toward the tip. This is called **foreskin**, and it can retract, or be pulled back, toward the base of the penis. The pulling back of that skin should not be forced and should be done by the person that has the penis. Typically, as the penis grows, and by the time a person is a tween, the foreskin can retract comfortably from the end of the penis. Some parents make the decision, while a baby is still a newborn, to have the foreskin removed through a surgical procedure called circumcision. Though it's usually not medically necessary to have the foreskin removed, there are many reasons that families around the world decide on circumcision. Sometimes it relates to a person's religion, their values, or the social norms of their culture.

── TRY THIS ──

Start a conversation to learn more about your family's values or opinions about circumcision. If there are people with penises in your home, what decisions were made and what influenced those choices? This conversation can be very different for every family. There's no one right answer.

The tip of a penis is called the **glans**. Remember when we learned about the glans of the clitoris? These two parts are homologous, meaning they are made of the same tissue and have thousands of nerve endings.

No matter how a penis forms or develops over time, all penises are amazing and should be respected!

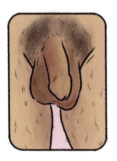  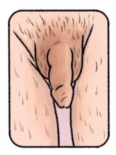 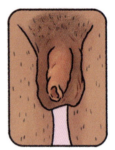

The **scrotum** is a sack of skin on the outside of the body under the base of the penis. Throughout puberty, the scrotum typically darkens in color, becomes larger and looser, and grows pubic hair. Inside the scrotum are the **testes** or **testicles**. During puberty, the testicles drop lower into the scrotum, begin to release hormones, and start to create sperm. The scrotum's job is to keep the testicles at the right temperature. If the testicles get too hot or too cold, it can become an incompatible environment for sperm to develop. If you have a penis, you may notice that your scrotum may tighten or shrivel up if your body is cold, or it may loosen or expand when your body is hot. When that happens, the scrotum is trying to protect the testicles.

People who have a penis are often born with two testicles, but not always. Some might be born with one testicle, or no testicles. Every body is unique!

> ### — FUN FACT —
> Sperm are among the smallest cells of the human body. They may look like tadpoles, but they don't turn into frogs. They are approximately two thousandths of an inch from head to tail. This means you would need a microscope to see them!

Millions of sperm can be produced in the testes each day, and they take around 65 days to fully mature before they travel into the **epididymis**. The epididymis is where sperm hang out until it's time for ejaculation. When this happens and it's time for the sperm and the semen to exit the penis, thousands of sperm receive the signal to begin making their journey out of the testicles. They travel from the epididymis through the **vas deferens**, which is a tube that wraps around the bladder. The sperm pass three different glands: the **seminal vesicle**, the **prostate gland**, and the **Cowper's gland**. These three glands are responsible for creating semen and pre-ejaculate fluid, which is whitish in color and travels with the sperm to help keep them nourished and moving along their journey through the **urethra** (the tube that pee travels through) and out the hole at the tip of the penis.

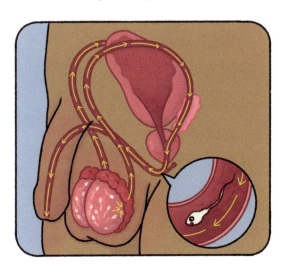

> **— FUN FACT —**
>
> Urine and ejaculate fluid both use the same hole to exit the body, but these two processes never happen at the same time. The body is super smart!

And finally, there's the **anus**, or butthole. During puberty, pubic hair often begins growing along the skin of the anus.

INTERSEX TRAITS

Some people are born with what are called intersex traits, meaning parts of their body (such as genitals, internal organs, chromosome patterns, or hormones) developed in ways that are not considered typically male or typically female. Here are some examples of what having intersex traits could look like:

* A person being born with both a uterus and a noticeably larger clitoris, which could look closer to the size of a penis.
* A person being born with internal uterine anatomy and no vaginal opening.
* A person being born with a penis and a scrotum that is divided in a way that looks more like labia.

Research shows that being born intersex is about as common as being a redhead. For some intersex people, the variations in their body aren't clear from the outside, so they don't realize they are intersex until later in life, such as when they go through puberty and their body changes (or does not change) in ways they weren't expecting. Or when they are adults and would like to have children but encounter unexpected challenges due to the variations of their internal reproductive parts.

> ── **TRY THIS** ──
> Watch a short video created by BuzzFeed featuring four people—Saifa, Pidgeon, Emily, and Alice—who share their experiences being intersex. Turn to page 155 and scan the QR code to find the video.

Some intersex tweens may have delayed or altered puberty experiences due to hormonal imbalances or differences in developing body parts. In some cases, medical interventions or hormone therapies may be recommended to align them with their gender identity or for their overall well-being. If you are intersex, you deserve affirming healthcare and support that honors your consent and helps you understand your body.

Unfortunately, a history of misinformation and discrimination has led to nonconsensual, unneccessary, and harmful surgeries having been conducted on intersex infants, children, and adults. Though many gaps still exist, increasing awareness and advocacy about being intersex is leading to greater protections for intersex children and adults. If you'd like to learn more about intersex traits, support, and advocacy, check out organizations like interACT, InterConnect, and the Intersex Justice Project.

If you have questions about how your body is developing, talk with a trusted adult and connect with an affirming medical provider. These are the best resources to support you as you're continuing to get to know your unique body.

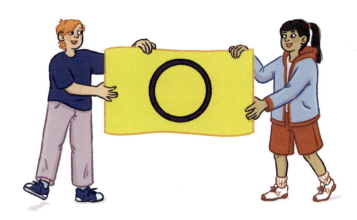

Real Questions, Real Answers

What is sex?

Sex is an activity that adults (and some older teens who feel ready) can do to feel pleasure, to bond, and sometimes to make babies. Sex is not something that kids do, because it's important to mature physically, mentally, and emotionally before making decisions about sex.

Even though sex is a natural part of the human experience, it isn't always a topic that people talk openly or comfortably about. You've probably seen or heard many different messages about sex from movies, books, songs, the internet and social media, or what friends or other people in your life have said about it. It's totally normal to have questions or to wonder about sex. Here are some important things you deserve to know.

* Sex happens when people bring their bodies together in ways that feel pleasurable; it's not just when a penis is inserted into a vagina, though that is one way sex happens.
* Sex should feel pleasurable and safe for everyone involved. If sex ever hurts or feels unsafe, the people involved should stop right away and check in with each other.
* Sex must involve consent. Consent means *permission*, and it is an ongoing agreement. This means if someone does not want to have sex anymore, it must stop, and just because the person wanted to have sex before doesn't mean they want to again. Sex should never be forced or pressured. (Learn more about consent, in nonsexual situations, starting on page 135.)

- Sexual acts without consent are called *rape*, *sexual assault*, or *sexual abuse*, which are all crimes.
- Sex requires trust and communication. If you're not able to talk about sex with someone, that can be a sign that you may not be ready to have sex with them.
- When sex is depicted in media or society, it is often represented as only happening between a woman and a man, in a heterosexual relationship, which is limiting and inaccurate. Sex is an experience that can happen between people of the same gender or between people of many different genders and sexual orientations.
- Not everyone wants to or chooses to have sex in their lifetime.

Various cultures, religions, and families can have different values and beliefs about what defines sex, when people are allowed to have sex, and even how to have sex. Even though it may be a while before you're making decisions about sex, it's important that you know facts and feel prepared to ask questions, so you can learn and be supported as you're growing up. For more information on sex and bodies that's designed for kids your age, I recommend checking out the books *Sex Is a Funny Word* and *You Know, Sex* by Cory Silverberg and Fiona Smyth. You can find more great resources like this on page 153.

Sexual pictures, videos, and online content are called **pornography**, or porn. Porn is made for adult entertainment, and it isn't a safe or reliable resource to turn to if you have questions about bodies or sex. Online porn can send confusing, toxic, and inequitable messages about bodies, consent, relationships, and sex. This can be harmful to young people who may think that these depictions are what's typical or expected within relationships or sex. While you're still learning about this stuff, it's important to stay safe and let a trusted adult know if you come across porn. It's their job to be available to have open conversations with you, answer your questions, and help you feel supported along your puberty journey.

Let's Write About It!

This section is just for your thoughts! Grab your notebook, paper, or device, and remember, there are no wrong answers.

* What words have you heard or been taught to use for body parts like the vagina, vulva, penis, or testicles? What words do you prefer to use when referring to these parts of your body?
* Our bodies do many amazing things each day that help us grow and experience life—like breathing, stretching, thinking, laughing, hearing, tasting, feeling, and so much more! Make a list of five to 10 things you are grateful your body can do.
* Now pick one thing from your list and think of something you can do this week to better support that activity or experience. (Example: I'm grateful my body can run long distances. This week I'm going to try to get more rest, so I feel recharged.)

Let's Talk About It!

With a parent, trusted adult, or friend, read these questions out loud and start chatting together.

* Which body parts and functions in this section did you already know about? Which were new to you or surprising? Which are you curious to learn more about?
* To ask a trusted adult: What's something you didn't learn about your body, or about bodies in general, until you were an adult?

Let's Have Fun with It!

Take the learning into your world by trying out this activity.

Let's get creative! Use molding clay or play dough to craft anatomy you've learned about in this section, like the vulva, uterus, ovum, penis, testicles, or sperm. As you create, remember that bodies, especially genitals, are diverse and unique in how they develop and change over time. Don't hesitate to make your own variations. It's also 100 percent okay, and totally common, if creating these crafts makes you giggle or even feel awkward. It's all a part of learning and normalizing these very human things.

Signs of Puberty

Now that we've covered some anatomy basics, let's go over the most common changes that bodies experience during the tween and teen years. Which changes you experience, and when, will unfold in a process that's unique to you. Having these facts can help you recognize what's happening to your body so you feel better prepared along the way.

Some of the changes described here may not apply to you yet, but you can revisit them when you're ready. Some of the changes may never apply to you, but I encourage you to read about those, too. Learning about puberty experiences that are different from your own is an important way to foster empathy, respect, and appreciation for others.

HAIR, HAIR, EVERYWHERE?

No matter your gender, you might notice new, slightly thicker hair growing on different parts of your body.

> **—— FUN FACT ——**
>
> Two types of hair grow on humans: **vellus hair** and **terminal hair**. Vellus hair (also called "peach fuzz") is the thin, shorter, and often lighter-colored hair that grows all over the body. Terminal hair is thicker, longer, and often darker hair that grows on certain parts of the body.

Before puberty, terminal hair typically grows on the scalp, eyebrows, and eyelashes. During puberty, rising hormone levels cause terminal hair to grow on other parts of the body such as the face, armpits, chest, abdomen, around the genitals and anus, and along the legs. This new hair has a few big jobs like regulating body temperature, keeping germs and debris from entering the body, and protecting the skin from harsh sun exposure.

It can be common for young people who have testes and/or higher testosterone levels to grow terminal hair on the upper lip, cheeks, chin, upper back, chest, knuckles, arms, and legs. Some young people who have ovaries and/or higher estrogen levels may also experience hair growth on some of these parts as well. Other factors, such as genetics and ethnic ancestry, also play a role in the way hair develops on the body.

Caring for Your Hair

You might be wondering how to manage this new hair, or you might prefer to let it flow and grow. Your family might also have certain rules, traditions, or expectations about body hair and grooming. There can be a lot to consider, and you should always have choice in the matter. If you're wanting to trim or remove any body hair, be sure to talk with a trusted adult so you have the right tools and don't hurt yourself in the process. Some of these tools include scissors made for trimming hair, razors and shaving cream or gel, and hair removal creams or wax. (For tips and techniques for trimming or removing body hair, go to page 89.)

Before making any changes to your body hair, think about your reasons why. Are you seeing body hair portrayed (or not) in different ways online, in media, or in your community? Have you received comments from others about your body hair? This can influence how you feel about the hair growing on your body. If you're feeling pressured to change the hair on your body, by others or by what you see online or in media, talk it out with a trusted adult or friend so you can feel clear about your decisions and the reasons for them.

NEW BREAST FRIENDS

No matter a person's gender, hormones typically cause the mammary glands to grow during puberty. Mammary glands—more commonly referred to as breasts, boobs, or chest—are made up of fat, tissue, nerves, and milk-producing glands. Breasts come in many different sizes, shapes, and skin tones, and it's common for each breast on the same person to be completely unique from the other!

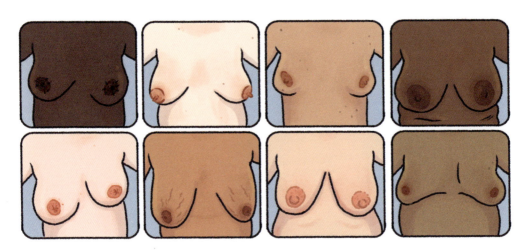

During puberty, early growth starts with the formation of small, button-like lumps called breast buds. If a person has more testosterone in their body than estrogen, breast development usually doesn't continue past the beginning stages of puberty.

Breasts have a nipple located at the center, surrounded by darker skin called the areola. Nipples are as unique as fingerprints. They grow to be many different colors, sizes, and shapes, and they aren't even the exact same on both sides of a person's body. Nipples can grow hair, and they can poke in or poke out. Some people have more than two nipples. This condition is called supernumerary nipples, and researchers estimate that around 200,000 people in the US have more than two nipples.

Breast growth can lead to soreness during puberty. Breasts can also become sore around the time of the menstrual cycle due to an increase in estrogen and progesterone, two hormones the body produces during a cycle. To help ease soreness during this time, drink plenty of water, eat nutrient-rich foods, and try to get extra rest. (For more on caring for your body during the menstrual cycle, go to page 95.)

Bras are a piece of clothing that some people wear to provide support to the breast area, or for style. They come in many sizes, designs, and shapes to fit different levels of comfort. The sizing systems can consist of letters (like XS, S, M, L, XL, XXL, XXXL, etc.) or a combination of numbers and letters (like 28AA, 32B, 36D, etc.) Sizing is based on measurements of the bust and band areas, which determine the cup size. Some clothing stores have people on staff who are trained to take these measurements for you and advise on the fit of your bra, which can be helpful for finding the right size and style. You can also try measuring your size yourself using a measuring tape and an online sizing guide. When shopping, be prepared to try on different options to see what feels right for you, and remember, the decision to wear a bra or not is totally up to you!

THE SKIN YOU'RE IN

During puberty, it's common to experience changes to the skin on your face, neck, and upper body due to the usual culprit: hormones! Sometimes these changes include bumps called acne (also known as pimples, or zits) and they can take different forms like blackheads, whiteheads, or cysts.

Having acne is super common—nothing to be ashamed of, and not a sign of poor hygiene. Our skin contains glands that produce an oily substance called **sebum**. This sebum is meant to keep our hair and skin naturally lubricated. Hormone shifts that happen during puberty can sometimes stimulate more sebum than is needed, which clogs the pores of the skin, traps bacteria, and causes pimples. Check out page 87 to learn ways to manage acne during puberty.

GAINS AND GROWTH

If you go to school or have a group of friends around your age, you've probably noticed a range of body heights, weights, and sizes. There's no one "right" height or weight. Changes to our height and weight during puberty are often called "growth spurts," and as a result of them, your bones, muscles, and fat will grow, strengthen, and distribute at different paces. If you ever have questions or concerns about the pace of your growth, be sure to talk with your trusted adult and pediatrician. They can help track your growth patterns and provide reassurance and support.

NOURISH AND MOVE YOUR BODY

Your body needs to be nourished to support all the growing it's doing during puberty, so you might notice yourself feeling hungrier at times. You may need more calories, protein, vitamins, and nutrients than you did before puberty started. It's important to listen to your body and fuel it with foods that will help build strong bones and muscles and keep you energized, like lean meats, vegetables, fruits, dairy (or dairy alternatives), whole grains, nuts, seeds, and beans. It's also important to stay hydrated by drinking plenty of water—around 64 ounces, or eight 8-ounce servings, each day.

In addition to balanced nutrition, it's important to include regular movement, exercise, and play in your life. These activities support your body's bone and muscle development and have a positive impact on your mental health, too. Playing a sport, riding a bike, going for a walk or roll, running, dancing, and doing yoga or martial arts are great ways to get your body moving. And just as important as being active, getting enough rest is vital to supporting your growing body and balancing your mood, mind, and energy.

During growth spurts, you might experience soreness or pain in your legs, called *growing pains*, especially if you are quite active or an athlete. Be sure to share with your trusted adults if the pain ever feels severe or frequent. Your pediatrician can help you better understand what is happening with your unique growth, too.

GOING DEEP

Did you know that voice changes happen to tweens and teens of all genders during puberty? These changes are often more noticeable if you have testes and/or higher testosterone levels.

Why does this happen? Your shifting hormones cause your larynx to grow longer and thicker. The larynx is in the throat, and it's responsible for creating the sound of your voice. Two vocal cords, made of muscle, stretch across the larynx like rubber bands. When you speak, air moves from the lungs and makes the vocal cords vibrate. This produces the sound of your voice. The pitch of the sound depends on how tightly the vocal cords contract as the air from the lungs passes through them.

When the larynx grows, it tilts at an angle inside the neck and sticks out at the front of the throat. This creates a bump of cartilage called the "Adam's apple." People with higher testosterone levels often have bigger Adam's apples because the larynx typically grows larger in their bodies. It's not just the larynx that grows during puberty; the facial bones, sinus cavities, nose, and throat area all get bigger too, which also contributes to different vocal sounds.

These voice changes typically happen between ages 11 and 14, though everyone's timing is unique. You may notice a cracking or breaking sound in your voice during the process, which usually lasts a few months. When the larynx is finished growing, those cracks stop and the new tone stabilizes.

Like many of the other changes during puberty, your voice cracking might feel uncomfortable, unwanted, or embarrassing. You may receive comments from family or friends as they notice what's happening. Remember that these changes are completely normal, temporary, and a sign that you are growing up!

GET A WHIFF OF THIS!

If you're thinking that changes during puberty really stink, well, you technically wouldn't be incorrect. Puberty literally causes new smells to develop on the body, which are often referred to as body odor, or BO.

The science behind body odor is actually pretty neat! Body odor happens during puberty because the hormone shifts cause the sweat glands to grow and produce more sweat, especially in areas like the armpits, genitals, and feet. These body parts have more apocrine sweat glands, which create sweat that contains fatty acids and proteins. But body odor isn't caused by sweat alone. Everyone has bacteria that naturally live on the skin, and believe it or not, those bacteria like to eat sweat. After they feast, the proteins they've consumed break down into acids that release a strong odor. That strong odor is what leads to BO. Basically, body odor is caused by bacteria farts!

Everyone has their own unique scent, and how much sweat your body produces can change depending on circumstance. The presence of bacteria on your skin, and within your body, is a natural part of keeping your body balanced—and sweat is helpful for regulating your body temperature. During puberty, bathing and using deodorant daily are two common ways to help regulate body odor and sweat. To learn more about hygiene practices to manage these aspects of puberty, check out page 89.

Let's Write About It!

This section is just for your thoughts! Grab your notebook, paper, or device, and remember, there are no wrong answers.

* Is there a puberty change you are looking forward to experiencing? Why?
* If you could skip one of the changes of puberty, which one would it be? Why?
* Pick one of the puberty changes mentioned in this section and create something to represent that change. For example: Write a poem or rap about body odor or pimples. Make a paper doll who is experiencing physical changes of puberty.

Let's Talk About It!

With a parent, trusted adult, or friend, read these questions out loud and start chatting together.

* Which puberty changes have you noticed or heard about other tweens or teens going through? This could be a sibling, friend, cousin, classmate, or even a character on a favorite show.
* To ask a trusted adult: Which body changes felt the hardest for you to go through when you were younger? What do you think could have made it easier on you?

Let's Have Fun with It!

Take the learning into your world by trying out this activity.

Get two rubber bands: one thin and one thick. Stretch each across two fingers. The rubber bands represent vocal cords stretched across the larynx. Now try plucking them. This represents the vibrations that occur when a person speaks, as air rushes from the lungs. What do you notice after plucking each one? The thicker rubber band makes a deeper, lower-pitched sound than the thin rubber band. This difference in sound is similar to how vocal cords work and change during puberty!

Puberty Across the Gender Universe

"Gender is a story, not just a word. There are as many ways to be a woman as there are women. There are as many ways to be a man as there are men. There are as many ways to be nonbinary as there are nonbinary people."
—Alok Vaid-Menon, poet, performer, and trans and nonbinary activist

Gender is an aspect of identity that can't be determined by another person, or by physical characteristics; only we know who we are and how we wish to express ourselves. As you're growing up, you might feel that the gender you were assigned at birth doesn't match the gender you know yourself to be. The changes that happen during puberty can cause feelings of **gender dysphoria** for some transgender, nonbinary, and gender-diverse tweens and teens, as well as young people identifying outside the binary. Gender dysphoria is a state of distress caused by feeling misaligned with the gender you were assigned at birth.

For example, if you have a uterus and identify as a boy, it might feel deeply disorienting when you start to menstruate, when you grow breasts, or when others expect you to act feminine. Or if you have a penis and identify as a girl, you might feel a sense of misalignment when your voice begins to deepen, when facial hair grows, or when people expect you to act masculine. Gender dysphoria goes beyond feeling uncomfortable with the changes of puberty; it can interfere with a person's mental health and daily life. Not all transgender, nonbinary, and gender-diverse young people experience gender dysphoria, but if this description feels familiar to you, it's important that you reach out to a trusted adult or provider of gender-affirming care, so you have resources and support. This section includes several options you can explore for finding support and alignment in your experience of gender.

Living outside the binary is not a new concept, nor is it a fad. For centuries, many cultures around the world have recognized and celebrated more than two genders. For example, the Diné people (also known as the Navajo people) have four genders, with the third called nádleehi, in which a person assigned male at birth embodies both the masculine and feminine spirit and takes on a mixture of masculine and feminine roles. The fourth gender is called dilbaa, who are persons assigned female at birth who take on masculine roles. Both dilbaa and nádleehi are people considered to be both masculine and feminine and are recognized as such by elders while they are still children. Navajo tradition places nádleehi and dilbaa in high esteem, and they have a historical role as healers and religious figures. In 1990, the term *Two-Spirit* was proposed and coined by Myra Laramee during the Third Annual Intertribal Native American, First Nations, Gay and Lesbian American Conference held in Winnipeg, Manitoba, Canada, to describe Native people who fulfill a traditional third-gender, or gender-variant, social role in their communities. Research shows that more than 150 different precolonial Native American tribes acknowledged third genders. What this gender expansiveness was called was unique to each tribe.

In Italy, there is a third gender called femminielli, who are persons assigned male at birth who dress as women and assume female gender roles. Until the nineteenth century, their status was considered privileged, and they practiced rituals based on

Greek mythology related to Hermaphroditus, an intersex child of the deities Aphrodite and Hermes, and to Tiresias, a male prophet of Apollo who transformed into a woman for seven years. In modern Italian society, femminielli are seen as good luck and have ritual functions within some Catholic celebrations.

In Hindu society, hijra is the most common nonbinary identity recognized in India. Their presence can be found in religious texts and within South Asian history. Many hijras are people assigned male or intersex at birth. They assume a religious role in celebrating rituals such as weddings and births. In the 1800s, British colonialism led to the hijra community being stigmatized and criminalized, but important progress was made in 2014: India's Supreme Court ruled to recognize a third gender, including hijras and transgender people, as citizens deserving of equal rights. If you are trans, nonbinary, or gender diverse, it's important for you to know that you are a part of a long history of celebrated people.

Another aspect of identity is **gender expression**, the physical representation of a person's gender through things like their clothing choices, hair, or personal style. In binary terms, it can relate to how feminine or masculine a person appears on the outside, but it can be a mix or neither of these. The idea that girls wear dresses, have long hair, and wear the color pink, while boys wear pants, have short hair, and wear the color blue is an example of a binary stereotype of gender expression. The truth is that a person of any gender can have any gender expression. Whether we're following gender norms or breaking them, how we express our gender can be a part of how we show ourselves to the world. We should all have the freedom to participate in gender expression in ways that feel most authentic to us.

As you explore your own unique gender and gender expression, consider the following ways you might find more alignment and affirming support.

Clothing: Regardless of your gender, consider how you feel in the things you wear, and give yourself permission to try new clothing you're drawn to. Though there's no actual need for clothes to be categorized by gender, they often are in our society. Try to view clothes with an open mind; if you like that dress or those basketball shorts, a bow tie, or the color pink, wear what helps you feel your most confident and comfortable.

Bras and underwear: No matter your chest or breast size, it is your choice whether you decide to wear a bra or not, and which style of bra you wear. Bras can feel affirming and comfortable to some people and not at all to others, so know that however you feel about bras is totally normal and should be supported.

The same thing goes for underwear and panties—the styles you wear should be your choice. Try not to restrict yourself to one type based on gender stereotypes. If you menstruate, know that there are companies now that make many different styles of period underwear, in various colors and patterns and in styles ranging from bikinis to boxer briefs.

Binders: These garments can be worn to compress your chest, if you have breast growth that you don't want to be visible. Just note that when using binders, it's important to give your chest a break from the compression. Be sure to wear them for no more than eight to 12 hours at a time, and not during high heat or while playing sports or exercising; excess sweating and moisture can cause irritation.

Packers: Packing can be an affirming option, particularly for transmasculine and nonbinary young people, if you want to have the appearance of a penis in your pants. There are companies that make products to support this. Many young people DIY it by placing a balled-up sock in their pants to create a bulge. Stand-to-pee devices (STPs) are another affirming option that allow people with vulvas to pee while standing. Some are in the shape of a penis, while others are funnel shaped. STPs can help you use a bathroom that aligns with your gender.

Makeup: Trying out different makeup types and application techniques can be an affirming experience. If you're unsure how to apply makeup, talk with a knowledgeable friend or adult, or find tutorials on YouTube from creators that feel affirming to you. Choosing not to wear makeup can feel like an affirming option, too.

Hair: Whether you keep it shaved, faded, short, long, or in braids, locs, twists, or other styles, the way you choose to wear your hair can be a form of gender expression and change how you feel within your body. And I'm not just talking about the hair on your head! The ways you choose to groom (or not) your facial hair, underarm hair, leg hair, and hair around your genitals can also affirm your most authentic self.

Alongside exploring your gender expression, here are several ways to connect with affirming people, providers, and spaces for support.

Share with an adult or friend who affirms you. Having a parent, family member, or close friend that you can talk to about your feelings—people who listen, believe you, and don't shame you—can be a meaningful part of belonging.

Consider your pronouns and ask for them to be respected. Gender pronouns are words or groups of words like *she/her/hers*, *he/him/his*, *they/them/theirs*, and *ze/zir/zirs* that are used in place of someone's name. For example: Owen uses they/them/theirs pronouns, so you might say something like, "I'm excited to get to see them again!" Jackie uses he/him/his pronouns, so you might say, "Let's send him a text and see what he wants to do." Consider how you feel about pronouns. Which, if any, help you feel like your authentic self? It's also possible to feel comfortable with multiple pronoun groups, or none at all. If the latter feels true for you, an alternative can be using your first name or a nickname in place of pronouns.

It's important not to assume someone's pronouns, as a person's gender expression doesn't always determine their pronouns. Asking them, especially when you first meet, is a good habit to form. This can sound like: "Hi, my name is Melissa. My pronouns are she/her/hers or they/them/theirs. What are your name and pronouns?" If you make a mistake and use a different pronoun, just correct it the next chance you get, to avoid **misgendering**. Misgendering means referring to someone by words or pronouns that do not reflect their gender. It can be hurtful and disrespectful, especially when done intentionally or without correcting oneself.

Your pronouns, whether they are the same as you were assigned at birth or not, are for you to explore and decide what feels most aligned with who you are today. When a parent, caring adult, or friend in your world makes a genuine commitment to learn and consistently use your pronouns, it is a loving act. Pronouns are not a preference. They can be an important aspect of who a person is and they should be respected. For more information about gender pronouns, including a helpful chart, check out the Glossary of Terms starting on page 156.

Connect with others in inclusive, gender-affirming spaces. Finding a sense of community, with other gender-diverse young people or with allies, can help you feel supported. Many schools have a gender and sexualities alliance (GSA) or queer student alliance (QSA), which are student-led clubs for LGBTQIA2S+ young people and allies to connect and experience meaningful activities together. (LGBTQIA2S+ is an acronym that stands for lesbian, gay, bisexual, transgender, queer, intersex, asexual, Two-Spirit, and other identities.) There are also community organizations like PFLAG, Gender Spectrum, and the Trevor Project that offer inclusive services, group support, and safe spaces online and offline for young people and their families. You can find more resources and information about these organizations on page 153.

Explore gender-affirming healthcare from knowledgeable providers. With the help of an adult you trust, finding a healthcare provider who offers gender-affirming care for adolescents is a valuable option—especially if you experience gender dysphoria during puberty. These providers can help you understand what you're going through, offer counseling services, and provide guidance on potential interventions. Puberty blockers, or medications that temporarily pause the progression of puberty, are one example of an intervention. This pause is not permanent, and it can give you time for self-exploration, counseling, and decision-making regarding future medical interventions, such as hormone replacement therapy (HRT) or surgeries. Puberty blockers can serve as a form of lifesaving care for trans and/or nonbinary young people.

Living as your most authentic self honors all those who have come before you. Feeling happiness, joy, and alignment in our gender identity and how we express ourselves in the world is referred to as **gender euphoria**. This feeling can be available to everyone, no matter your gender.

Real Questions, Real Answers

I know I'm nonbinary, but my family has always called me a girl and expects me to act feminine. I want to tell them and not feel like I'm hiding. How can I share my gender with them?

Deciding to share that you're nonbinary is a deeply personal experience that can bring on a mix of feelings such as excited, scared, unsure, free, nervous, and proud. Sharing your identity, particularly when it is different from what others have perceived you to be, is often called *coming out*. Though there's no one "right" way to come out as nonbinary, here are some steps to consider.

1. **Reflect for yourself.** Make sure you have a good understanding of what being nonbinary means to you. This will help you talk about your experience and feelings to your family and answer questions they might have.

2. **Choose how you'll share.** Pick the communication method that feels most comfortable and safest to you. For some it might be writing a letter, email, or text. For others it might be talking in person. If speaking face-to-face, try to find a distraction-free, comfortable setting where you can have an uninterrupted conversation. Plan for ways to feel more comfortable in your body if the conversation gets hard, like taking breaths, using a fidget toy, or holding a comforting object.

3. **Be honest and direct.** You can start the conversation by expressing how much their support means to you. Then, clearly state that you identify as nonbinary and explain what that means to you. It might mean you tell them your pronouns, the name you prefer to be called, or examples of what makes you feel affirmed in your gender. Share your experiences and let them know that this is an important part of who you are.

4. **Share resources.** Your family might have questions or need more information about nonbinary identities. You can share resources like books, videos, articles, or websites that can help them learn. The resources section of this book starting on page 153 has several great options, including organizations like Gender Spectrum, the Trevor Project, and PFLAG.

5. **Communicate your boundaries.** Let your family know what kind of support you need from them and what kind of language and behavior is respectful to you as a nonbinary person. Remember that it may take time for them to fully understand your identity, and they may need space to process their own feelings.

6. **Seek support.** After you come out, connect with a friend, another family member, or a trusted adult who you feel safe to talk with—someone who is ready to celebrate with you if it goes well or comfort you if it does not.

After you share your identity, it may take some time for your family to digest what this means, do further research, ask questions, and change how they address you. They might need to practice your new pronouns or name. They might make mistakes. Let them know when this happens or if you feel your boundaries have been crossed in any way. People who respect and care about you will understand, work on correcting any mistakes, and show their support.

It's also important to know that you don't have to come out if you don't want or feel safe to do so. Not telling someone that you are nonbinary or transgender isn't lying or hiding the truth. If you do want to come out, you get to decide when and to whom. You get to decide what is best for you. Above all, remember that coming out is a personal journey, and it's okay to take things at your own pace. Trust yourself and know that you are valid and deserving of love and acceptance, no matter what.

Let's Write About It!

This section is just for your thoughts! Grab your notebook, paper, or device, and remember, there are no wrong answers.

* In what ways do you express your own gender?
* Write about something that has helped you, or could help you in the future, feel a sense of gender euphoria.
* Write about a time you felt more comfortable presenting in ways associated with a different gender.

Let's Talk About It!

With a parent, trusted adult, or friend, read these questions out loud and start chatting together.

* Share about a time you felt truly seen and accepted for who you are.
* To ask a trusted adult: Think back to your childhood and the gender norms you experienced. How have gender messages changed or stayed the same since then?

Let's Have Fun with It!

Take the learning into your world by trying out this activity.

* Check out a short video by the online magazine *Them* to hear transgender tweens and teens describe their experiences growing up. Scan the QR code on page 155 for the link.
* Explore the history of gender expansiveness around the globe by checking out "A Map of Gender-Diverse Cultures." Scan the QR code on page 155 for the link.

"We have the power to change the narrative of body shame in our lives. We are not bound to the tales of teasing and criticism we were subjected to as children. The good news is we are the authors of our own lives."

—Sonya Renee Taylor, best-selling author, social justice activist, poet, and founder of The Body Is Not an Apology

PART 3

How Do I Take Care of My Body During Puberty?

About Body Image

It's common to begin to wonder if your body is "normal" or "good enough," particularly during puberty. All of the changes and outside influences can cause your body image and confidence to fluctuate—especially if others are noticing the changes and pointing things out in ways that feel uncomfortable. Many messages we receive through television, movies, and social media portray biased and unrealistic standards about body size, shape, and what's considered "healthy."

Your **body image** is how you think and feel about your body. The way our culture portrays and talks about bodies makes it easy to compare your body to those of others, which can lead to negative self-talk and a fixation on standards that are often not realistic. But you deserve to accept yourself as you are! When you feel good about your body, you're more likely to take care of it and feel good about yourself overall.

How can you maintain a positive and accepting body image during puberty? Here are some tips to practice.

Unfollow and unsubscribe. Whether you're watching a movie, scrolling social media, shopping, gaming, or reading a book or magazine, different types of media often send messages about bodies and beauty standards that are not realistic or healthy. For this reason, it's important to be aware of the media you consume. On top of the tendency to idealize certain types of bodies and features, some media representations may not even be real. Companies and individuals alike can use photo-editing software to digitally manipulate, filter, and edit images. Don't hesitate to unfollow, unlike, unsubscribe, and disconnect when you see or hear something that causes you to question your own body or that presents an unrealistic representation of others' bodies.

Follow diverse media and positive role models. Take notice of the types of shows, characters, or content creators you watch most. Are they representing many different viewpoints, life experiences, identities, cultural backgrounds, body types, and genders? Or are they representing a lot of the same perspectives and people? Too often, entertainment media and social media algorithms are designed to elevate content that shows white, thin, able-bodied, and heteronormative people and experiences. At the same time, algorithms often suppress content made by and about disabled people, fat people, LGBTQIA2S+ people, and Black, Brown, Indigenous, and people of color. This is totally unfair, and you don't have to fall for it! When using social media, be sure to like, comment on, share, and subscribe to the work of diverse creators. This will direct the algorithm to show you more content just like theirs. Connect with media and role models that represent realistic, diverse, and healthy examples of the many ways bodies and people can be.

Don't turn to online pornography or sexualized media when you're curious about bodies. Online porn often shows unrealistic, unhealthy, harmful, and confusing messages about bodies, relationships, consent, identities, and sex. This kind of media is made for adults, not for young people, and it's created for entertainment, not for education. If you want to learn about these topics, talk to a trusted adult who can help guide you toward honest answers and reliable resources made for people your age. For example, amaze.org offers videos for tweens and teens to learn all about bodies and sex in age-appropriate ways. You can also check out the resources list starting on page 153 for more great options created just for young people.

Choose not to talk about other people's bodies. Making comments about other people's bodies is unnecessary at best, and rude or hurtful at worst. Even if you think you're paying someone a compliment, you don't know how your comment will be received, and it may have a harmful impact on someone else's body image and self-esteem. For these reasons, it's best not to comment on other people's bodies at all. This includes not asking questions or making assumptions about the bodies of transgender, nonbinary, and/or gender-diverse people. If you have a friend or family member who frequently comments on or makes jokes about other people's bodies, change the subject or directly let them know that you aren't okay with this. If that doesn't work, consider spending less time around them.

Think about who benefits when you don't like or accept your body. (Hint: Not you!) Did you know that billions of dollars are made each year by beauty companies and social media influencers who rely on consumers to think that they need the next new diet, workout routine, or piece of clothing to feel and look good? They try to convince us that we are not attractive/cool/interesting enough as we are, and that we *must* buy this or that product to make it all better. Basically, they make a profit from shaming and manipulating people. The truth is, there is not one "right" way for a body to be, and so-called beauty standards are always changing. What's considered "hot," "in style," or the quick fix today will be considered "out" tomorrow. Find your own style, and let what feels good to you be your guide. It will save you lots of money and heartache!

── TRY THIS ──

Next time you're getting ready in an outfit, accessories, or hairstyle you've picked, take a moment to notice the feelings you're having while rocking the look. Think of the first word that comes to mind. If the word is something positive, then that style choice is likely a keeper. No outside or second opinion needed! If the word is something negative, you may want to reconsider. Ask yourself: *Why am I choosing this if it doesn't feel right for me?* Try something different that gives you all the good feels.

Celebrate your whole self! It's natural to think about your body in terms of how it looks, especially as it's going through changes, but don't neglect the rest of yourself. Your talents, personality, sense of humor, and interests are important parts of what makes you *you*, and focusing more on these aspects can help balance your body image. Celebrate the amazing things your body can do and the ways you nourish your body. How you talk to yourself plays a big part in this. If you're not sure where to start, the activities on page 85 can help.

You only have one body, and it's the same body that is with you during both the difficult and the amazing moments of your life. Spend time getting to know and care for it, so it can also care for you along the journey. In Part 4, you'll learn helpful tips and activities to support your self-care and healthy habits. If you ever have questions or concerns about your body image, talk to your trusted adult, a medical provider, or someone else you trust for support.

Let's Write About It!

This section is just for your thoughts! Grab your notebook, paper, or device, and remember, there are no wrong answers.

* Name one thing you can do if you're ever feeling less confident about your body—for example, practicing affirmations, moving your body, journaling, or talking through your feelings with a friend.
* Write about a time you felt confident about your body. What were you doing, and what helped you feel confident? Were you by yourself or with someone else? If a memory does not come to mind, describe what would help you feel more confident about your body.
* Think of someone who you admire for qualities other than their physical appearance, such as their personality traits or unique talents. This could be a person you know or it could be someone you've seen and not met yet. Share a little about what you look up to or relate to most about them.

Let's Talk About It!

With a parent, trusted adult, or friend, read these questions out loud and start chatting together.

* What messages have you noticed coming from people around you, social media, or entertainment about bodies and beauty standards? Have these messages impacted how you think about your own body?
* To ask a trusted adult: When you were a tween or teen, did you ever feel pressure to have your body look a certain way? How did you handle it?

Let's Have Fun with It!

Take the learning into your world by trying out this activity.

Make a playlist of your favorite songs that help you feel confident and powerful. Play it, dance, or move your body to it anytime you need some positive vibes! If you'd like some inspiration, check out this playlist of songs that tweens and teens of our Growing Into You!™ puberty workshops love. Turn to page 155 to scan the QR code and follow a link to the Spotify playlist.

Hygiene Hacks

Without even realizing it, you probably have plenty of habits in place to take care of your body each day; brushing your teeth, washing your hands, and bathing your hair and body all count! During puberty, as hormone shifts cause your body to change, your hygiene habits become even more important for staying healthy. Let's go over some tips for the most common habits.

MANAGING ACNE

Having pimples is a common part of puberty, thanks to the surges of hormones that result in more skin oils that can trap bacteria in your pores. Acne is not shameful or a sign that you're not hygienic. In fact, influences that are totally outside of your control, like genetics and the environment, can trigger acne flare-ups. You can be a five-star face washer and still experience breakouts. But acne can be uncomfortable, and you may be looking for tips to manage it. Try these:

* Wash your face in the morning with a mild, fragrance-free soap and cool to warm water. Try to cleanse gently rather than scrubbing, so the skin is not irritated.

* Wash your face at night before bed, too, and take care to wash off any products you may have used on your face, like makeup or sunscreen. Washing at night will prevent these products from building up and clogging pores.
* Wash your face after exercising or sweating heavily.
* Apply a moisturizer daily, moments after you shower or wash your face. Moisturizing skin while it is still wet allows for better absorption because the skin is porous. Be sure to hydrate from within as well, drinking at least eight 8-ounce cups of water daily.
* Hair care products, especially ones that contain oils, can sometimes clog pores along your hairline, forehead, or back of your neck. If you notice breakouts in these areas, try switching to an oil-free product.
* If you're having breakouts on your face, try using products labeled *noncomedogenic* or *nonacnegenic*, which mean they are designed to not clog pores.
* When you notice a pimple, try with all your might not to pick at or squeeze it. Messing with pimples can cause them to become more irritated and inflamed—as you could be introducing new bacteria from your fingers to the area—and it can even lead to scarring.

If you experience breakouts, pay attention to when they happen and how long they last. It's common to notice pimples around the time of your menstrual cycle, if you have one, due to hormone shifts. Some people notice breakouts after they've eaten certain foods. If this happens, consider taking a break from the food to see if your skin improves. You may have a sensitivity or intolerance.

The truth is, you could do everything "right" and still experience breakouts, so try to be patient with your body's puberty journey. Sometimes it is helpful to see your pediatrician or a dermatologist so they can examine your skin and determine if a treatment—like a certain medication, cream, or change in habits—is needed to better support your skin's health.

BALANCING BODY ODOR

If you're feeling a big N-O toward BO, first let me be clear: it is totally normal for your body's scent to change during puberty. Hormone shifts cause sweat glands to grow and produce more sweat, especially in areas that are now growing hair, like the armpits and genital area. Sweat isn't just there to be annoying—it actually helps regulate your body temperature! Your personal hygiene routine may take a little more time and effort now, but if you're concerned about sweat and body odor, there are lots of ways to manage these parts of puberty.

* Bathe or shower daily with a mild, antibacterial soap to cleanse the skin and remove bacteria that can contribute to odor. Pay attention to the areas on your body that are prone to sweating, such as the armpits and genitals. After bathing, thoroughly dry these areas to reduce moisture and minimize bacterial growth.
* Wear breathable, loose-fitting clothing when possible, especially if you're in hot weather or being active. Clothes made of cotton or linen are best for allowing air circulation and can lessen sweating.
* Use deodorant daily to help control sweat production and mask odors. Be sure to look for products that are free of ingredients like aluminum, paraben, baking soda, or artificial fragrances, as these can cause irritation.

THE HAIRY TRUTH

Some people prefer to remove or trim their body hair, while others choose to let their natural hair grow and flow. A person's choices can be influenced by social norms or expectations, cultural traditions, or what feels most comfortable or pleasing to them.

If you choose to shave, talk with a trusted adult first to make sure you have the right tools and techniques to stay safe in the process. The same goes for waxing, trimming, and using hair removal creams. It's also worth noting that some body parts, like the genital area, can experience itchiness and irritation when hair that has been removed begins to grow back. Think carefully about your hair grooming decisions to make sure they feel like the right choices for you.

Tips for Shaving

* Choose a razor with clean, nonrusted, sharp blades. If you're shaving hair on your face, you might prefer an electric razor over a manual razor.
* Pick a shaving gel or shaving cream that can help the skin stay moisturized and limit friction during shaving. Look for products that contain ingredients such as aloe vera, vitamin E, oatmeal, or shea butter.
* To begin, wet the skin with warm water, which helps open the pores. Some people choose to shave while they're in the shower, especially when shaving body parts like the underarms, legs, or genital areas.
* Apply shaving gel or cream to the body part you're shaving. Then press the razor to the skin and glide across using gentle, slow strokes, moving in the direction that the hair is growing. Shaving in the opposite direction of the hair growth can cause irritation and rashes called *razor burn*.
* Rinse your razor between every few strokes to clear the blades of shaving product or hair.
* Some parts of your body—like the curve of the underarm, knee, upper lip, chin, and neck area—are trickier to shave. For these areas, try to stretch the skin or

bend or straighten the body part in a way that can make a flat surface that allows the razor to glide more easily.
* Keep in mind that cuts and nicks can happen while shaving. When they do, use a clean tissue or cloth to apply direct pressure and stop the bleeding.
* When you've finished shaving, rinse the area with cold water to help calm the skin and constrict the open pores. Some people use aftershave, which is a cream, oil, or liquid designed to tighten the pores and seal minor cuts. Try to avoid ones with artificial fragrances, which can irritate or dry the skin.

Remember, everyone's body hair and skin are unique, so it may take some trial and error to find what works best for you. The decision to groom body hair during puberty is a personal one, and it's important to prioritize your comfort, safety, and how you want to express yourself—while respecting other people's choices, too.

KEEPING GENITALS CLEAN

Skin and hair—down there—also need daily cleansing. I'm talking about the vulva area, penis, scrotum, and anus. You should wash these areas at the same time you're washing the rest of your body. Be sure not to use harsh or fragrant soaps that can strip the skin of its natural moisture and cause irritation, like dryness, itching, or rashes. Simply rinsing with water alone is often enough, or you can use a mild soap. If you have an intact penis—meaning it did not experience circumcision—be sure to clean the outside of the penis and beneath the foreskin. This will prevent bodily fluids, dead skin cells, and bacteria from getting trapped in the area.

If you have a vagina, remember that it cleans itself, so do not insert soaps or products to try to "clean" that area. The natural fluids the vagina makes each day (called discharge, secretions, and cervical mucus) are designed to keep the vagina healthy and clean. These fluids have natural odors that are unique to each person.

possible vaginal fluid colors

Vaginal fluids are usually clear or whitish in color. If they ever appear greenish, yellowish, or thickened like cottage cheese, or if they have a strong or different odor than usual, let a trusted adult know. This can be a sign of infection, which a medical professional can diagnose and provide treatment for. Vaginal infections are common and nothing to be ashamed of!

No matter which genitals you have, if you ever experience discomfort, frequent itching, pain, burning sensations while peeing, or other concerns with these body parts, talk with a trusted adult or your pediatrician.

Overall, to make hygiene easier to manage during puberty, remember to drink plenty of water, eat nutrient-rich foods, stay active, and try to get consistent rest. Your body is working hard as it grows!

Let's Write About It!

This section is just for your thoughts! Grab your notebook, paper, or device, and remember, there are no wrong answers.

* Think about the norms and expectations that exist in your family, culture, or religion related to body hair. Write about the influence this expectation has had on you or others in your community.
* Imagine you are competing in the Hygiene Olympic Games. Which hygiene habit would you be most likely to win a gold medal in?
* Choose one hygiene habit you would like to improve and list the steps you can take to help you be successful.

Let's Talk About It!

With a parent, trusted adult, or friend, read these questions out loud and start chatting together.

* What's one hygiene habit you'd like to learn more about?
* To ask a trusted adult: Think back to when your body was going through puberty. Did you ever feel embarrassed about the changes your body was going through or that you needed to start certain hygiene habits?

Let's Have Fun with It!

Take the learning into your world by trying out this activity.

Create a hygiene plan that fits your schedule. To start, think of the hygiene habits you routinely practice from the time you wake up to the time you go to bed. Use the following examples to help you create your list:

- Showering/bathing
- Brushing your teeth
- Flossing your teeth
- Washing and moisturizing your face
- Applying sunscreen
- Putting on deodorant
- Eating a snack or meal
- Doing your laundry
- Taking care of your nails
- Shaving
- Washing your hair
- Sleeping

Now write out a schedule, marking when in your day you practice each habit. Some will be a part of your daily schedule, while others you complete weekly or monthly.

When you've finished creating your hygiene plan, think about ways you can stay on track. You might schedule reminders on your device for certain habits or create a sign that you can hang up. And once you've completed a habit that you've been working toward, you can think of a fun way to celebrate yourself, like doing a happy dance or enjoying a special treat.

Remember, your hygiene routine is unique to you! Creating a plan can help you improve or maintain the habits that keep your body healthy during puberty.

Period Power!

"I think getting a period is like having a superpower!"
—Sam, 9 years old

A period. Aunt Flo. That time of the month. Surfing the crimson wave.

Whatever you call it, menstruation is a totally natural bodily process, yet our society still doesn't do a great job of talking honestly or positively about it. Let's change that!

If you aren't having periods, or never will, learning about menstruation isn't something to skip over. Here are a few big reasons why:

* Menstrual cycles play a major role in reproduction, which means that without periods, we as humans would not exist. So, we gotta give thanks and respect to this powerful process!
* Over half of the world's population has a uterus and may menstruate in their lifetime. That's a lot of people!
* Chances are high that there is at least one person in your life who has menstruated in the past, menstruates now, or will menstruate in the future. Being informed about this experience can help you practice empathy and feel more comfortable supporting friends and people you care about.

Let's start with some basic facts:

People with uteruses typically have a first period between ages 8 and 16. The very first period is called menarche (pronounced "MUH-naar-kee"), which comes from two ancient Greek words: μήν (mēn) meaning "month" and ἀρχή (arkhē) meaning "beginning."

Periods are a natural monthly cycle, triggered by hormones like estrogen and progesterone, which send signals between the brain, ovaries, and uterus to complete four distinct phases. The fluid that comes out of the vagina during a period is made up of blood, cells, tissue, and mucus, which are created each month in the uterus. This fluid is the uterine lining, which would remain in the body if the person became pregnant and would protect the fertilized ovum (egg). When a person is not pregnant, the lining leaves the uterus through the vagina. This shedding of the lining usually takes three to seven days.

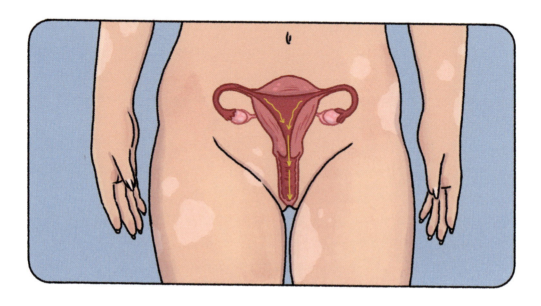

Though it may seem like a lot of blood and fluids are leaving the body with each cycle, the total amount is actually five to nine teaspoons. Menstrual care products like pads, a cup, tampons, and period underwear can be worn to absorb or collect the fluids, instead of the blood landing on clothes or bedding. (We'll cover more about period care products starting on page 104.)

While the bleeding phase of the menstrual cycle is what we usually think of when we talk about periods, there's much more to this cycle, which usually lasts between 27 and 33 days when a person's cycle is regulated. Understanding the four phases and various shifts in hormone levels unlocks menstruation's powerful purpose. Let's break it down.

MENSTRUAL PHASE

This phase is when the period occurs, and it's considered the start of the cycle. During this phase, a person might feel cramping, bloating, more tired than usual, and shifts in mood. The body is working hard! During this phase, it's important to eat nourishing foods, hydrate, and get lots of rest. Cramping typically lasts for one to two days at the start of the period and is the result of the uterus contracting to loosen the uterine lining. Some ways to relieve discomfort or pain from cramping are to:

* apply a heating pad or warm compress to the abdomen area
* stretch or move your body in a nonstrenuous way
* take an over-the-counter pain-relieving medication
* take a warm bath
* rest your body

If cramping ever lasts for longer than a couple days or feels so painful that it's difficult to do your typical activities, talk with someone you trust or a medical provider for support.

——— TELL ME MORE! ———

Sometimes painful, prolonged cramping or other unpleasant symptoms can be a sign of uterine fibroids or conditions such as endometriosis, polycystic ovary syndrome (PCOS), or premenstrual dysphoric disorder (PMDD). These are not commonly diagnosed in the tween years, but it's good to be aware of them as you grow.

Uterine fibroids are noncancerous growths that occur inside or around the uterus. They can vary in size and can change the shape of the uterus. Symptoms can include heavy or long menstrual periods, pelvic pain, urinary or bowel issues, and pain in the back and/or legs.

Endometriosis is a condition in which tissue that's similar to uterine lining grows in areas outside of the uterus, such as the ovaries or fallopian tubes, which can cause increased menstrual pain, abnormal vaginal bleeding, and chronic pain in the lower back and pelvis.

Polycystic ovary syndrome (PCOS) is a condition in which the ovaries produce an imbalanced amount of androgen hormones, which can cause symptoms such as irregular periods, excess hair growth, acne, and infertility.

Premenstrual dysphoric disorder (PMDD) is a condition that happens during the luteal phase of the cycle (see page 99), causing severe symptoms of depression, irritability, anxiety, and tension.

FOLLICULAR PHASE

This is the second phase of the menstrual cycle, when eggs in the ovaries are preparing for release. During this phase, more estrogen is produced by the ovaries and the uterine lining thickens. This boost in hormones can cause a person to feel more energized and creative during this phase.

OVULATORY PHASE

During the third phase in the cycle, the egg (or sometimes eggs) is released and begins to travel through the fallopian tube toward the uterus. For people with a uterus who are sexually active, this phase is the time when fertilization and becoming pregnant is possible.

LUTEAL PHASE

This is the last phase, when the egg lands inside the uterus. The uterine lining is at its thickest, which is needed if a person becomes pregnant. If the person is not pregnant, the ovum dissolves within the lining and the cycle begins again with the menstrual phase! During the luteal phase, a person might feel big shifts in mood due to the fluctuating hormones progesterone and estrogen. These shifts are often collectively called PMS, which stands for premenstrual syndrome. If you ever hear negative comments about mood swings or jokes that you're "PMSing" during this time, you can flip the script and say, "No, it's just being luteal!" It's all part of a powerful, natural process.

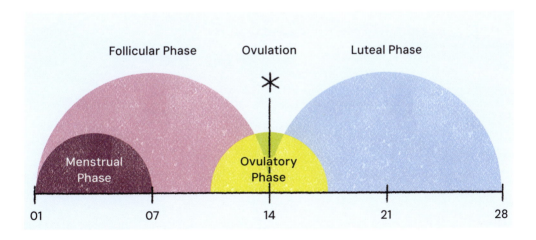

> **— FUN FACT —**
>
> After a person has their first period, it can take up to five years for their cycle to regulate, so try not to be alarmed if your first few years of monthly bleeding seem inconsistent.

Aside from the bleeding, mood shifts, and possible cramping, the hormone fluctuations during menstrual cycles can also bring about symptoms like headaches, pimples, and period poops. Period poops are caused by an increase in prostaglandins, which are hormone-like substances in the body that relax the muscles of the bowels in the same way they relax the muscles of the uterus to help it shed its lining. Period poops can include diarrhea, abdominal pain, bloating, and/or constipation. This most commonly happens near the beginning of the cycle, but it could happen within the other phases as well.

If you have periods, a great way to get to know your unique body and menstruation journey over time is through period tracking. This can be as simple as writing in a calendar each day of a month, recording information such as the following.

* Was there menstrual bleeding? Yes or No
* If yes, how was the flow: light, medium, or heavy?
* List any symptoms you experienced (examples: cramping, bloating, headache, period poops, pimples).
* Write one to three words to describe your mood and physical state today (examples: tired, creative, bloated, annoyed, confident).

You can also use a period tracker app for a digital experience that provides daily prompts to help you document your menstruation journey. Be sure to talk with your trusted adult if you are interested in trying a digital option, and choose an app that allows you to maintain your privacy.

If you have questions about menstruation or about your unique period journey, be sure to talk with someone you trust or a medical provider, so you feel prepared and supported.

Let's Write About It!

This section is just for your thoughts! Grab your notebook, paper, or device, and remember, there are no wrong answers.

* If you menstruate now or are expecting to menstruate in the future, make a list of ways you would like to be supported by others during your period.
* If you aren't expecting to menstruate, make a list of ways you can support the people in your life who do menstruate. Here are a few examples to get you thinking: offer to shop with them to buy period care products; be a good listener if they need to talk during their cycle; make a commitment to not talk negatively about periods.
* How have you noticed periods being talked about (or not talked about) in your family, at school, and in the media? Write about what you've observed.

Let's Talk About It!

With a parent, trusted adult, or friend, read these questions out loud and start chatting together.

* Why is it important for menstruation to be a topic everyone can talk openly about?
* To ask a trusted adult: Growing up, how did you learn about periods? How were periods talked about in your home, school, and in the media?

Let's Have Fun with It!

Take the learning into your world by trying out this activity.

Have you ever seen a movie that focuses on the topic of menstruation? If not, here's your chance! Prepare your favorite snack, and watch *Period. End of Sentence.*, an Academy Award–winning documentary short film about a group of young people from Los Angeles, California, who get inspired to make a positive difference in the lives of menstruating people in the Indian village of Kathikhera. Turn to page 155 and scan the QR code to watch the movie on YouTube.

Period Care

Let's be real. Periods can sometimes cramp your style. What if your period leaks onto your bedding or gets on your clothes? How do you keep your period from getting in the way when you're at school? Don't worry. There are a lot of options available to help manage your flow.

Even if you aren't menstruating right now (or never will), this section is super important for better understanding the different choices, considerations, and opportunities out there for taking care of periods and the people who have them.

You might have seen period care products in grocery stores, public restrooms, school bathrooms, or your own home. Some of these may be labeled as "feminine" hygiene products. That terminology is limiting and harmful since having a period is something a person with a uterus can experience, regardless of whether that person identifies as masculine, feminine, both, or neither. Period care is for everyone who has a period. It's that simple!

If you've ever wondered *How do period care products work?* or *Which one is best for me?* I've got you! Check out this guide to five different period care products.

PADS

Also called sanitary towels or sanitary napkins, pads come in disposable and reusable forms and are worn outside the body. Their job is to absorb menstrual flow.

How to use: Pads attach to the inside of underwear, beneath the vulva. Some disposable pads have sticky "wings" to assist in staying attached and catching leakage, while other types of pads rely solely on a sticky backside instead of wings. Disposable pads must be placed in the trash after use. Reusable pads are made of cloth and should be washed after each use. Instead of a sticky backside, they typically have wings that can be secured to each other with a button. Pads come in different absorbency levels for lighter and heavier flows, and there are also pads designed to be worn overnight during sleep. Depending on flow, pads should generally be changed every three to five hours during the daytime.

Positives: Pads are usually simple to use and don't require insertion into the vagina. They can be worn overnight without negative effects. Compared to other period care products, pads are often easier to find in stores or public restrooms. Reusable pads are designed to be environmentally friendly and can be a cost saver in the long run—and they can come in fun patterns and designs, like cartoon sharks and colorful stripes!

Challenges: Pads may result in leakage if they shift out of place, aren't changed frequently enough, or are the wrong absorbency level. Some people may find them uncomfortable to wear. Pads also cannot be worn with some types of underwear, like thongs or loose-fitting boxers, and they cannot be used during activities such as swimming. Reusable pads, when they need to be changed for a clean one, may feel challenging to deal with when not at home. (Pro tip: Bring a small washable bag with you to store worn reusable pads.)

LINERS

Liners, or panty liners, come in reusable and disposable forms, and are worn outside your body. Their job is to absorb menstrual flow.

How to use: Liners are similar to pads, but thinner and meant for lighter flow. Like pads, liners attach to the inside of underwear. Some liners have wings, while others only have sticky backing. Disposable liners must be thrown away after use and should be changed every three to five hours depending on flow. Reusable liners are made of cloth and must be washed after each use.

Positives: Great for lighter-flow days, liners are thinner and may be more comfortable to wear than pads. Similar to pads, they can be worn overnight and don't require insertion into the vagina. Like reusable pads, reusable liners can be cost-effective in the long run and environmentally friendly.

Challenges: Liners will not absorb as much as pads and may result in more leakage if they are not changed often enough or if they shift out of place. Some people may find them uncomfortable to wear, and they cannot be worn during activities like swimming.

PERIOD UNDERWEAR

Also known as period panties, period underwear is meant to be worn on the outside of your body, like standard underwear. They are reusable. The portion touching the vulva area is specially created with multiple layers of both waterproof and absorbent materials* designed to absorb menstrual flow.

How to use: Period underwear is worn like regular underwear and washed after each use. It comes in different absorbency levels, including underwear that are designed for overnight use. Period underwear can be worn up to 12 hours a day, depending on flow and the absorbency level of the underwear. Each pair should be replaced every one to two years.

Positives: Period underwear is designed to be comfortable to wear and leak-proof. (But as with pads, if the underwear isn't changed regularly, leakage can occur.) And, like reusable pads, they can be cost-effective over time and environmentally friendly. Period underwear also comes in a variety of fun designs, colors, and styles, such as high waisted, bikini, boy short, and boxer brief.

*Note: When shopping, look for period underwear that is free of PFAS, PFOS, and PFOA, which are chemicals that are harmful to the human body.

Challenges: It can be somewhat costly to stock up on period underwear, although it can be a money saver in the long run. As with reusable pads, period underwear requires washing and drying and may not be convenient to carry with you when not at home. On heavier flow days, there is a higher chance of feeling some dampness. And like other period care products worn externally, they cannot be used when swimming.

TAMPONS

Tampons are disposable and commonly made from cotton and/or synthetic materials. They are inserted into the vagina to absorb menstrual flow.

How to use: Tampons come in different absorbency levels, such as light, regular, and super. Choose a tampon with an absorbency level that matches your current flow. Most tampons come with an applicator that helps with insertion. Tampons are inserted into the vaginal canal using this applicator, after which the applicator is disposed of. (This can be tricky to learn at first—don't 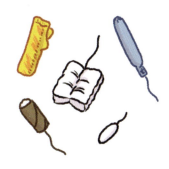 be afraid to ask a trusted adult for advice! Instructions are also included in the tampon box.) Tampons can be worn inside the vagina for three to six hours, depending on flow. After each use, the inserted absorbent part of the tampon is removed and thrown away. It's important to change tampons regularly to avoid toxic shock syndrome (TSS), a rare but serious infection that can occur when a tampon stays in for too long, or when a higher absorbency tampon is used on a lighter flow day. A liner can be worn in addition to a tampon to prevent leakage.

Positives: Some tampons can hold more menstrual flow than pads, depending on the absorbency level. Compared to period care products worn outside the body, there is a lower risk of odor during use. Tampons can also be worn with many different types of underwear and during activities like swimming.

Challenges: Inserting tampons takes practice and may be uncomfortable or challenging to get used to. And for trans and nonbinary people, wearing tampons may trigger gender dysphoria. Because tampons carry a higher risk of vaginal infections and irritation, it's important to change tampons regularly and use tampons that are free of plastic, polyester, polypropylene, fragrances, and colorants. In addition, they should not be worn overnight or during very light flow. Compared to reusable products, tampons are cheaper in the short term but less cost-effective in the long run, and like other disposable products, they are not environmentally friendly.

MENSTRUAL CUPS AND DISCS

Cups are reusable and commonly made of silicone or latex. Discs come in reusable and disposable forms. Their job is to collect menstrual flow. Menstrual cups and discs are worn internally, inside the vagina.

How to use: Menstrual cups and discs have a bit of a learning curve when it comes to insertion, but the package they come in should have instructions. You can also seek advice or find tutorials on the brand's website. There are different techniques for inserting a menstrual cup, which usually involve folding the mouth of the cup. After insertion into the vaginal canal, it expands and opens to collect menstrual flow, creating a seal against the vaginal walls. This prevents leaking until the seal is broken, when the cup either overflows or is removed. Cups can be worn for up to 12 hours, depending on flow. To remove, carefully pinch the base of the cup to break the seal and pull downward. Once taken out, the cup can be emptied and then cleaned with hot water and soap. To avoid infection or irritation, wash the cup with clean hands and make sure the cup is clean before reinserting it. Depending on the brand or material, the menstrual cup may need to be sanitized in boiling water every month. Menstrual discs are similar to cups, but they have a shallower design and can be inserted further into the vaginal canal. Disposable discs should be thrown away after use. Reusable discs can be cleaned like menstrual cups.

Positives: Like other reusable period care products, reusable cups and discs are environmentally friendly and cost-effective in the long term. They can be worn for a longer period of time than other products, and they carry no risk of TSS when used and cleaned properly. They can be worn during activities such as swimming.

Challenges: Cups and discs may be harder to learn how to use, especially for first-time menstruators, and it may take some time to get used to how they feel when inserted. Reusable cups and discs require proper cleaning and maintenance to avoid irritation and infection.

Every period product takes a little bit of practice and getting used to. These products can also help you learn more about your own body and what feels right for you. If you have questions about period care products, be sure to talk to someone knowledgeable that you trust.

TRY THIS

Now that you know more about period products, consider making a period kit that can help you—or a menstruating person in your life—feel prepared and supported during a cycle. Select a small bag or pouch for this kit and put in the following items.

* A few menstrual care products. Pads are a great choice for first-time menstruators.
* An extra pair of underwear. (Note: If you're making a period kit for someone else, let that person fill the bag with the underwear of their choice.)
* A smaller sealable bag for storing used underwear or reusable period products
* Disposable wipes or tissue
* A small bottle of hand sanitizer
* A note with an encouraging doodle or message, like "You rock!" or "You've got this!"

If you're ever in a pinch and need a period product, it's okay to ask. Many people carry extra disposable ones with them and are often happy to share with someone in need. Grocery stores and drugstores are good places for a quick shopping trip to restock, too.

PERIOD CARE TIPS FOR TRANS, NONBINARY, AND GENDER-DIVERSE MENSTRUATORS

For some people, having a period can cause feelings of gender dysphoria, discomfort, or anxiety, due to how our society has historically linked menstruation with girlhood and womanhood. But it's important to remember that having a period is *not* what makes someone a girl or a woman. People of any gender can have a period, as long as they have a uterus, vagina, and ovaries that menstruate.

If the experience of menstruation is causing feelings of dysphoria or discomfort, here are a few tips to try.

* **Find the period care products that you feel most comfortable using.** This might mean using a product that you don't have to insert, or one that you can wear longer without having to change as frequently, or a product that doesn't make a lot of noise when changing it in a public restroom.
* **Pick products that feature gender-neutral marketing and design,** instead of products that rely on gendered stereotypes. Reusable pads and underwear may be helpful, since these products tend to have a wider range of styles and designs, such as period underwear in a boxer-brief cut. If purchasing period products online is an option for you, this may be more convenient and less stressful than shopping for them in a store.
* **Experiment with ways to affirm yourself during menstruation.** Wear clothes that feel comfortable and that align with your gender expression.
* **Use the restroom that affirms your gender (if it's safe to do so).** Look for single-occupancy or gender-neutral bathrooms, which provide more privacy. If using public restrooms designated for men, you may notice that the stalls do not always have trash bins. To work around this, you can wrap the used product in toilet paper and dispose of it when you get to a trash can.
* **Track your period.** You can use a calendar, a planner, or an app to help you keep track of how you're feeling and where you are in your cycle. This can help you notice patterns and be prepared for when your period comes. (If using an app, look for one that prioritizes consumer privacy and uses gender-inclusive language.)
* **Practice self-care.** Try to get good rest and protect your peace, to keep stress levels low, during this time. Staying hydrated and eating nutrient-dense foods like fresh fruits and vegetables are also helpful ways to minimize period symptoms. If you do experience cramping, try applying a warm water bottle or heating pad to the abdomen or lower back area for relief.

* **Connect with people in your life who support you.** This may look like texting with your friends, joining a LGBTQIA2S+ group for tweens and teens, or talking to a trusted adult. Surrounding yourself with people who support and care about you is always a good idea. And if you have concerns or questions about your experience with menstruation, let a trusted adult know.
* **Talk with a trusted adult about gender-affirming care.** There are medical options for pausing or stopping your period, such as puberty blockers, which can be explored with the help of a gender-affirming healthcare provider.

Real Questions, Real Answers

Does using a tampon or menstrual cup mean that you've lost your virginity?

This is a common myth. First of all, tampons and menstrual cups are for managing period flow. They have nothing to do with sex or virginity. Second of all, virginity, or the concept of being a virgin, is an idea that refers to someone who hasn't had sex. This concept can mean different things to different people, and for some people it means nothing at all. Whether someone has had sex or not doesn't define their value. It is never okay to shame someone for their sexual choices—or, for that matter, what period care products they use!

Can I pee if I'm wearing a tampon?

Yes! Since the tampon is inserted into the vaginal opening, not through the urethral opening (where pee comes out), you can pee while using a tampon, as well as a menstrual cup or menstrual disc.

Does everyone with a period use period care products? Are there people who just let it flow?

Great question! Menstruating without using period care products is called *free bleeding*. During free bleeding, the blood and uterine lining flows freely onto the person's clothing, a towel, or folded-up sheets of toilet paper, instead of being collected or absorbed by a menstrual care product. Some reasons people free bleed include:

* They prefer the experience of menstruating without using products.
* It can be more affordable.
* They want to protest period shame or stigma. Free bleeding has been used as a powerful statement to bring awareness to normalizing menstruation and menstrual health education.
* They want to minimize waste in landfills created by using disposable period care products. Free bleeding has also been used as a statement in support of the environment.
* It's their only option when period products are not accessible.

Free bleeding generally requires some planning ahead, such as wearing absorbent clothing or underwear or making use of towels. Though some people prefer using period care products to free bleeding, it's important to know it exists and is one way people manage their periods.

How do I know which period care option to choose or recommend?

Every menstruator has different priorities and reasons for choosing the period care product they use. Common factors include:

* What's available
* What feels easiest to use
* What feels most comfortable or safest
* What is most affordable
* What feels the most gender-affirming
* What helps connect people to their cycle (for example, inserting and removing menstrual cups may help someone get to know their vulvar area and period)

Regardless of the reason, the choice should be up to the menstruator to decide what is best for their body. Just because one option works for a friend or a family member doesn't mean it will work for someone else. It's also totally okay to experiment with different period care products over time as your body, flow, and lifestyle change.

Period Poverty

Did you know that period care products (and education about periods) are not accessible or affordable to everyone? This issue is known as *period poverty*, and studies show that it affects an estimated 500 million people worldwide. In 2018, New York became the first state to require that free menstrual care products, such as pads and tampons, be made available to students in public schools. Since then, just half of the states in the United States have passed similar laws.

This problem doesn't just affect girls and women. Transgender, nonbinary, and gender-diverse people with uteruses also can encounter barriers when trying to access period care products. These barriers may take the form of feelings of gender dysphoria, or facing discrimination, harassment, or abuse from people who hold harmful, inaccurate beliefs and stereotypes about gender.

There's also the issue of the *period tax*, also known as the *tampon tax*. This refers to laws that add a sales tax to the cost of period care products when they are purchased in stores—instead of treating period care products as nontaxable items, like other basic necessities. This additional sales tax can make period care products less affordable for people who need them. In May 2023, several period product companies such as August, Cora, DIVA, Here We Flo, the Honey Pot, LOLA, Saalt, and Rael joined forces to stand against this unjust practice. They created the Tampon Tax Back Coalition, which reimburses consumers for any amount of tampon tax paid on their products.

> ──── **TRY THIS** ────
>
> * Become a period pro and learn even more about menstruation by checking out books like *Red Moon Gang: An Inclusive Guide to Periods* by Tara Costello and *Go with the Flow* by Karen Schneemann and Lily Williams.
> * Research the laws impacting menstrual equity in your area by visiting periodactionday.com/advocacy.
> * Host a period care product drive in your school or community. For a complete list of helpful steps to get started, go to periodactionday.com/service.

The more informed we all are about menstrual health and period care products, the better we can advocate for changes that ensure everyone has period care access, education, and support.

Period Care Products Throughout History

Though many options are available today for managing periods, this hasn't always been the case. Let's take a trip back in time and check out the journey many period care products have taken to evolve to what we see today! Knowing this history can help us better appreciate how far menstrual care has come.

Ancient Egypt (circa fifteenth century BCE): Water-softened papyrus was inserted into the vagina, much like a tampon.

Ancient Rome: Wool was inserted into the vagina to absorb menstrual flow.

Medieval times: Rags were used as pads. Some people wore the ashes of toads over their abdomen, believing that this would relieve cramps.

1800s (and earlier): Homemade cloth pads were created from woven fabric or flannel.

1860s to 1870s: The first prototypes of menstrual cups, also known as catamenial sacks, were patented. A catamenial sack was inserted into the vagina, and a cord attached it to a belt worn around the waist. These never made it to market.

1880s to 1890s: The Hoosier sanitary belt was marketed, and available to those who could afford it, as an elastic waistband with clips to hold a sanitary napkin in place.

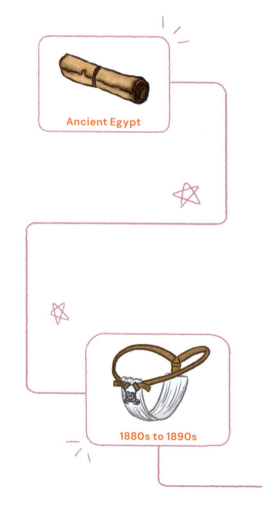

Ancient Egypt

1880s to 1890s

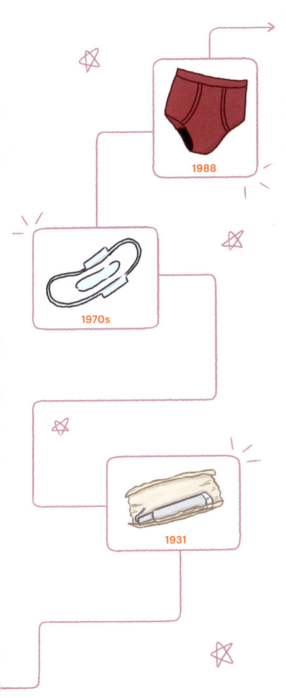

If you could invent a product to support menstruators, what would you create?

2017: Period blood was shown in a commercial for the first time, instead of the blue-colored liquid that companies had used previously, causing a shame-busting shift in how periods are represented in the media.

1988: The first patent for period underwear was filed.

1970s: Adhesive pads became widely available.

1957: Mary Beatrice Davidson Kenner, a Black American woman, invented and patented the first belt to secure pads in place while wearing them.

1937: Leona Chalmers, a white American actress and author, invented the first menstrual cup made of vulcanized rubber.

1931: Dr. Earle Haas, a white American physician, patented the first cotton tampon with an applicator. He got the idea from a friend who inserted sponges into her vagina during menstruation. He designed the applicator so the cotton would not have to be touched when inserted.

1921: Kotex began marketing a disposable pad in women's magazines.

1897: Johnson & Johnson pioneered the first mass-produced disposable pads sold in the US.

Period Care Products Throughout History

Let's Write About It!

This section is just for your thoughts! Grab your notebook, paper, or device, and remember, there are no wrong answers.

* Which period care product would you feel most comfortable using, and why?
* If you've had your first period, share what you remember about the first time. Where were you? What feelings did you have? Did anyone give you advice or support you?
* Based on what you've learned, what advice would you give to someone else to help them with their first period?

Let's Talk About It!

With a parent, trusted adult, or friend, read these questions out loud and start chatting together.

* Do you have concerns or fears about any of the period care products described on pages 104–109? What would make you feel more comfortable trying a new period care product?
* To ask a trusted adult: Which period care products do you remember learning about when you were growing up? Which products were the most easily accessible? What do you wish someone had taught you about period care products?

Let's Have Fun with It!

Take the learning into your world by trying out this activity.

Next time you're at a grocery store or drugstore, find the period product section. Write about the following questions in your journal or talk about them with someone you trust.

* Which period care products do you see? Which are not available here?
* What do you notice about the products in front of you? For example, the differences in pricing, the quantities available, how they are marketed, and the location of the products in the store.
* Do you notice any gender stereotyping used in the way the products are marketed or displayed within the store?
* What, if anything, would you change about what you see in order to make the products more accessible and inclusive?

Bonus Activities

* Pick out a period care product to purchase either for yourself or to keep in your home for guests who menstruate.
* Buy a few period care products to donate to a local reproductive health organization, your school, or another community organization.

Planning for Self-Care

Sometimes our culture talks about self-care like it should be a trendy or exclusive experience, like a spa day or a vacation—only available for special occasions, or if you have a lot of money. Thankfully, that's totally untrue! Self-care is about how we nourish ourselves—our minds, bodies, and spirits—in everyday life. Developing self-care practices during puberty can help you learn how to take good care of yourself for years to come.

Check out this Wheel of Self-Care. Which are you already incorporating into your puberty journey, and which could you add or try?

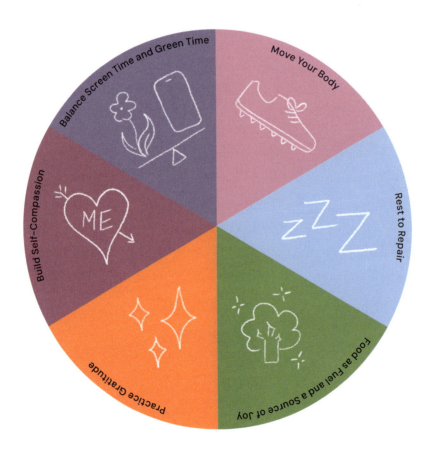

MOVE YOUR BODY

Regular physical activity has many benefits during puberty and throughout life. It supports your developing bones, muscles, and heart health; manages stress; improves coordination; regulates sleep; and gives a boost to your mental health as it releases endorphins (the brain's feel-good neurotransmitters). And you don't have to be a competitive athlete to benefit from regular movement; a daily walk through your neighborhood, a dance party with friends, swimming in a pool, or shooting baskets at the park all count! Choosing activities you enjoy is the best way to consistently incorporate movement into your life.

REST TO REPAIR

Believe it or not, your body is doing important work while you rest. During sleep, the brain releases essential hormones needed for bone and muscle growth. Rest improves brain function, memory, and emotional regulation. Throughout your puberty years, try to get around eight to 10 hours of sleep each night. A consistent nighttime routine can help with this and gives you something to look forward to in the evening. Try taking a shower or bath, followed by a low-stimulation activity like reading a magazine or book, writing about your day in a journal, or listening to relaxing music. (It's best to avoid screen time before bedtime, as the short-wavelength light from screens can mess with your sleep cycle!)

FOOD AS FUEL AND A SOURCE OF JOY

The food we eat can have a big impact on our physical and mental health. Food not only helps us grow, it can be a positive way we connect with friends and loved ones. During snacks and mealtimes, try to incorporate nutrient-rich foods like fresh fruits and vegetables. Getting adequate protein, fiber, calories, carbohydrates, and vitamins from foods like meats, vegetables, fruits, dairy, whole grains, nuts, and beans can help build strong bones and keep you energized. Finally, stay hydrated by drinking at least eight 8-ounce cups of water daily. To help with this, you can bring a refillable water bottle with you to drink at school, during activities, and while using devices.

PRACTICE GRATITUDE

Gratitude helps us focus on the positive aspects of life so that we better recognize our strengths, celebrate our achievements, and acknowledge the support we receive from others. Gratitude doesn't fix everything, of course, and it's okay to be honest about what's hard as well as what's good in your life—but starting a regular gratitude practice can help you notice what you appreciate rather than fixating on what could be better. Try writing down three things per day that brought you joy. You could even invite a friend to join you in your new practice!

BUILD SELF-COMPASSION

Puberty can be a vulnerable time for negative self-talk, criticism, and comparison, all of which can lead to feelings of insecurity and self-doubt. Practicing self-compassion means treating yourself with kindness and acceptance, especially when you make mistakes or are feeling unsure of yourself. Self-compassion allows you to embrace your mistakes as learning opportunities, and to recognize that you are worthy of every good thing in life, exactly as you are.

BALANCE SCREEN TIME AND GREEN TIME

Though screens and social media are an integral part of today's world, overusing them has negative effects on our bodies, minds, and mental health. Set reasonable limits to create balance between your time online and time spent IRL. Find ways to learn and be creative without screens, like reading, journaling, drawing, a sport, or a fun hobby. Make space in your schedule for *green time*—time you spend connecting with nature—by going outside, feeling the sunlight and fresh air, and observing the sights and sounds of nature. When you are online or using screens, choose content that's safe, positive, informative, and made for people your age.

Self-care is a lifelong journey. It's common to experiment with different practices and approaches, as what works for you this week might need to shift to something new next week. If you ever have questions about any aspect of your self-care, or if you need help balancing the stressors in your life, talk with a trusted adult or medical provider so you have support.

Let's Write About It!

This section is just for your thoughts! Grab your notebook, paper, or device, and remember, there are no wrong answers.

Make a list of five to 10 things that you love about yourself. Use the following prompts to jump-start your thoughts:

* I love that I am . . .
* I love that I can . . .
* I am happiest when I . . .
* I am proud of myself for . . .
* A unique thing about me is . . .
* Think about a self-care practice you enjoy. What do you like most about this activity?

Let's Talk About It!

With a parent, trusted adult, or friend, read these questions out loud and start chatting together.

* What's one self-care practice you would like to try?
* To ask a trusted adult: Think about how you take care of yourself now. What's one self-care practice you could try or do more regularly as an adult?

Let's Have Fun with It!

Take the learning into your world by trying out this activity.

Create a self-care calendar for the next one to three months. Include activities you do now and activities you want to start adding into your daily, weekly, or monthly life. They can be as simple as reading a book, looking up at the sky, or looking at old photos of friends and family.

As you plot your activities on the calendar, think about any supplies, support, or steps you may need to turn your plans into reality. Use the calendar below for inspiration.

JULY

		1 Daydream	2 Write in a journal	3	4 Play an instrument	5 Cook or bake
6	7 Talk to a friend	8 Listen to music	9	10 Play a game with someone	11	12 Draw, paint, or create art
13 Play with a pet	14	15 Paint my nails	16 Dance	17 Watch a movie	18 Plans with a friend	19 Visit the library or bookstore
20 Do a puzzle	21	22 Write a poem	23 Play a sport	24	25 Try something new	26 Take pictures of nature
27 Volunteer in my community	28	29 Go for a walk or roll	30	31 Take a nap		

"I try to build a healthy self-image and surround myself with people I can trust."

—Tyson, 14 years old

PART 4

How Can I Connect with Myself and Others During Puberty?

Exploring Pleasure

What if I told you that your brain and your body work together to allow you to experience pleasure? This can happen in everyday moments, like when we enjoy the smell of freshly baked cookies, or go outside and feel the sun on our skin, or when we spend time with someone we appreciate. Pleasurable experiences can prompt the release of **dopamine** (one of the neurotransmitters we learned about in Part 1), which sends signals through the body that make us feel good. When we can notice what feels pleasurable to our bodies, we can also recognize when something does not. This awareness keeps us safer and better able to care for our bodies and overall well-being.

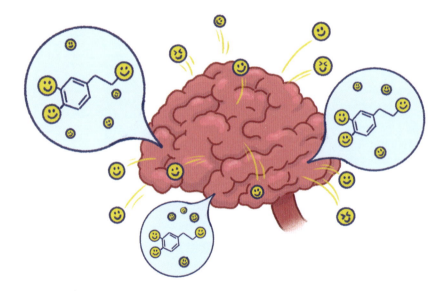

Pleasure can also happen through **masturbation**, which means touching your own body—typically parts of the genital area, like the clitoris or penis—for pleasure. Unfortunately, this subject isn't always talked about openly because there can be a stigma attached to it. But contrary to what you might have heard, there's nothing weird, bad, or wrong about masturbation. (And no, it does not stunt your growth, or cause pimples and hairy palms, or lead to blindness!) Masturbation is a natural way to get to know your own body—what feels good to you and what doesn't.

As you learned in Part 2, these parts of the genital area are packed with thousands of nerve endings, which means that they often feel good when touched or when rubbed against something. You may already be trying this, or you may be curious about it, or you may just not be interested. Some people masturbate often and some not at all. All of these choices are perfectly okay.

If you do decide to masturbate, there are a few important things to remember.

* **Masturbation is an activity done in private.** It's not something you do in public or around other people. Private spaces like the bathroom or your bedroom when you're alone are usually good options.
* **Clean your hands before and after masturbating.** Wash your hands with soap and water to ensure that you don't introduce germs to these sensitive body parts, and that you don't accidentally transfer your bodily fluids to where they aren't meant to be. Use clean items like washcloths, towels, tissues, or toilet paper when wiping away fluids.
* **There's no one "right" way to masturbate, as long as it's done safely.** To get a baseline understanding of your body, try a body scan exercise. With nonjudgmental curiosity and in a private space, take a look at your body in a mirror. It can be a large mirror or a handheld mirror. With clean hands, see how different parts of your body feel as you explore them. What sensations do you notice? What feels comfortable and safe? What does not? Listen to your body and trust what works for you. Also, while your body is still growing your hands are the safest tools to use during masturbation. Though you may have heard about sex toys or vibrators, these are tools made for adult bodies. It's best to wait until you're older, and your body has fully developed, before introducing these options.

Getting to know your own body is a powerful way to connect with yourself and feel more comfortable expressing boundaries, especially if you decide to invite anyone else to get to know your body when you are older. It can also help you notice when something about your body causes you discomfort or concerns you in some way. For some people, touching their genitals can feel uncomfortable or cause feelings of gender dysphoria. It's important to pay attention to your body and only do what's comfortable for you.

Let's Write About It!

This section is just for your thoughts! Grab your notebook, paper, or device, and remember, there are no wrong answers.

* What does pleasure mean to you?
* How do you experience pleasure in your everyday life?
* Draw a picture of something or someone that brings you joy.

Let's Talk About It!

With a parent, trusted adult, or friend, read these questions out loud and start chatting together.

* Masturbation and pleasure are topics that people aren't always comfortable talking about. Why do you think this is?
* To ask a trusted adult: Growing up, how was the topic of masturbation treated in your family or community?

Let's Have Fun with It!

Take the learning into your world by trying out this activity.

We can experience pleasure in many ways in everyday life. Point to the ways you enjoy experiencing pleasure.

Sing a song	Write a poem	Take a walk, ride, or roll
Hang out with a friend	Smile	Watch a funny movie
Play a sport you love	Play a board game	Listen to music
Cuddle with a pet	Enjoy a favorite food	Call or text with family
Volunteer	Play an instrument	Play outside
Draw	Bake	Read a book

Practicing Consent and Boundaries

In its simplest definition, **consent** means permission, and it shows up frequently in our everyday lives, like when you're asking someone to hang out or when you're borrowing something from a friend. But it's important to deepen the definition of consent to mean not just permission but an agreement between people that involves communication—verbal or nonverbal—and respect.

Boundaries are rules set by you that help you feel safe and respected in interactions and relationships with others. Boundaries can be physical, emotional, and even digital. Some examples of personal boundaries can be not sharing hugs with people you don't feel comfortable hugging, carving out time to yourself when you need a break, or unfollowing online content that makes you feel uncomfortable.

Both consent and boundaries are necessary aspects of healthy relationships and healthy interactions with others. They are life skills that take practice.

Imagine this: You're playing a game with a friend, and after you win the game, you raise your hand in the air to invite them in for a high five. The friend sees this, smiles,

and raises their open hand as well to meet yours with a clap. Without using words, you've both agreed to share in a high five. This moment of agreement is an example of nonverbal consent, where two people agreed to do something together. You both used affirming body language through your hands and facial expressions to "say" what you meant.

Now imagine the same example, but instead of no words being exchanged, you ask for consent by raising your hand and saying, "Can I get a high five?" Your friend says happily, "Yeah!" followed by the high five. This time, consent was shared verbally.

Verbal consent can also be written. This might be when a contract or permission slip is signed. For example, parents review and sign consent forms for their child when they take them to a medical appointment. These forms give permission for their child to receive healthcare and to allow certain health information to be shared with other providers, when needed. Once you become an adult, you'll take over the task of reviewing and signing consent forms at your own medical appointments.

But what if you want to give someone a high five and they leave you hanging? They don't raise their hand to meet yours—or, in other words, they don't consent to a high five. What would you do? Would you demand a high five, or act offended? Or would you accept their decision and move on? After all, just because someone high-fived you in the past doesn't mean they'll always want to—and when someone does not give their consent, it must be respected without teasing, trying to change their mind, or giving them the cold shoulder.

The rules of consent are especially important when talking about bodies. Your body belongs to you, and no one else is entitled to your body; at the same time, you are not entitled to anyone else's body. For example, if someone goes in for a hug and you don't feel like being touched, this is a moment to set a boundary. That could sound like saying "No, thanks!" or putting your hand out for a shake instead of a hug, if you're comfortable with that.

To consent to something, it must feel clear what you're agreeing to. If you're ever unclear, you can ask the other person directly. And if you or someone else changes their mind or does not give consent, that must be respected.

Remember that everyone has different boundaries and comfort levels. Let's say you're playing a game of football in the park with your friends, and you know that in your family, you tackle when someone has the ball. But your friend isn't comfortable with that and prefers touch or flag football. Your friend's comfort level should be respected. Again, it's good to pay attention to both verbal and nonverbal communication about how people are feeling.

If someone touches your body in a way that violates your boundaries or just doesn't feel right, move away from the situation to create space and safety, and then talk to someone you trust. Remember, it is never your fault if someone violated your boundaries or consent. You never deserved or asked for it.

Ultimately, setting and communicating your boundaries takes practice, and even when you feel you've got it down, there still may be certain situations or certain people where boundary setting feels less comfortable. This is often because of power dynamics or social expectations, like when the person wanting the hug or kiss is an older relative such as your grandparent, aunt, uncle, or parent. You may feel less able to say no to them, especially if you're growing up in a culture where it's expected that you greet elders with physical affection, regardless of whether you truly want to or not. In these situations, it can help to talk about your boundaries with someone you trust before you anticipate the dilemma happening.

For example, before going to a family event, think about the ways you want to handle greetings. Would you rather wave, say hello, offer a hug, smile, fist-bump, or do something else? Then practice letting someone know your boundary, like: "Hi, Grandpa! I don't feel comfortable with a hug or kiss today. I'm happy to see you, though! How have you been?" Practice creating space by taking a step back if your verbal boundary is ignored. The more you practice these skills, the more confident and prepared you can feel. And don't hesitate to ask for help or backup if needed from someone supportive who is present.

── TELL ME MORE! ──

It's not your job to make someone feel more comfortable with your boundaries, especially when that someone is an adult. They are responsible for managing their reactions and feelings. Setting your boundary honors your comfort and safety and gives the other person an opportunity to learn and grow from the experience, too.

How can you practice communicating your boundaries and respecting the boundaries of others?

As you get older, you may begin making decisions about physical relationships and sex. It's important to understand that consent is a necessary part of any form of intimate touch. Sexual activity should never be attempted with someone who expresses discomfort (verbally or nonverbally), someone who does not understand what is happening, someone who is under the influence of alcohol or drugs, or someone who changes their mind. Sexual activity without consent is called rape, sexual assault, or sexual abuse. These are all crimes. Understanding consent, before it has anything to do with sex, is an essential way to practice the skills, communication, and awareness that keep you and others safer.

Consent is also about knowing what you *do* want or feel comfortable with, so I encourage you to practice speaking up for yourself without believing that you're selfish, picky, or high-maintenance. Examples of this are saying "I love this song! Can you turn it up, please?" or saying "I need a hug right now. Would you be able to share one with me?" Knowing what you want, and understanding what you deserve in life, is powerful. Your *yes* is just as important as your *no*!

If you ever have questions or tough situations related to consent, talk with someone you trust so you have support along the way.

Let's Write About It!

This section is just for your thoughts! Grab your notebook, paper, or device, and remember, there are no wrong answers.

* Write the letters C-O-N-S-E-N-T down the side of a page. Next to each letter, write a word or phrase related to consent and boundaries that begins with that letter. For example: for *C* you could write "communicate" or "cannot be forced."
* Think about the last time you said no to someone. What did setting that boundary feel like? How did the person react? Write about it.
* Journal about what you might say or do in a moment when your consent or boundaries are not respected. Feel free to design your response in a creative way, such as writing a script, drawing it as a comic, or writing it as lyrics to a song.

Let's Talk About It!

With a parent, trusted adult, or friend, read these questions out loud and start chatting together.

* On a scale of 1 to 10 (with 1 meaning *not at all* and 10 meaning *extremely*), how comfortable do you feel saying no or setting a boundary at home? How about with your friends? At school? With certain family members? Talk about the ratings you gave to each situation and any challenges that could show up.
* To ask a trusted adult: Share about a time growing up when your boundary or consent was not respected. What did that feel like? How did you handle it? How would you handle it now, knowing what you know about consent?

Let's Have Fun with It!

Take the learning into your world by trying out this activity.
Read each of the following scenarios and decide whether it is an example of practicing consent or if you think consent is missing.

1. You go into your older sibling's closet looking for something to wear. You find a shirt you like, take it, and wear it to school.

2. You just heard that your closest friend is moving to another city. Your dad notices you are feeling sad about the news. He asks you, "Would you like a hug?"

3. You arrive at a family get-together and are introduced to an aunt that you met once when you were little. You politely smile at her. She reaches her arms out wide, comes toward you, and pulls you in for a big hug.

4. Your friend gives your phone number to a new kid at school without asking you first if it's okay.

5. You're eating dinner with your family, and your mom sees that you finished your plate. She asks if you'd like another helping. You say, "No, thanks." She says, "Okay," and doesn't pressure you to eat more.

Bonus Activity

For every scenario where you thought consent was missing, what could be done differently to make it an example of practicing consent? Share the scenarios with a friend or someone you trust. See what answers and thoughts they come up with.

Being a Good Friend During Puberty

We've learned how important it is to have solid support during puberty. Now let's talk about what it means to *be* a solid support and a good friend to others during these years. The following qualities of a good friend were suggested by tweens in our Growing Into You!™ virtual puberty workshops (they're spot-on!).

A good friend is someone . . .

* you can trust
* who is honest with you
* you have fun with
* who doesn't talk about you behind your back
* who stands up for you
* who likes to spend time with you
* who shows you respect
* you can laugh with
* who apologizes when needed
* who is a good listener
* who respects and calls you by the name and pronouns you use
* you can be yourself around
* you can relate to
* who is kind
* who likes to see you happy
* who makes time for you
* who is fair
* who shows you forgiveness

What do you think of these qualities? Which ones feel most important to you in your friendships? Which ones do you work hard to demonstrate to your friends? What qualities would you add to this list?

Sometimes friendships during puberty can feel complicated. As you're growing and changing, so are your friends. You might have disagreements or develop different interests. There may be times when you feel really connected and other times when there's distance.

Following are three examples of friendship dilemmas. Read each one and then answer the questions: *What do you do? How could you be a good friend?* Below each scenario are helpful tips and possible solutions to guide you through your answers.

SCENARIO 1

You see a few of your friends crowded around a phone and laughing. You ask to see what they're laughing at, and they show you a video of Erika, another classmate, drooling while sleeping on the bus. Your friend Jamie says he took the video this morning and wants to post it on social media. *What do you do? How could you be a good friend?*

Consider the facts: Jamie is not being respectful or using good judgment. Jamie should not have taken the video of Erika without her consent, and he should not be sharing it with others. These kids are not being good friends, and they could face big consequences for their choices.

Ways to be a good friend: Being honest with Jamie, even if that means having a hard conversation, is a way to be a good friend. First, you decide not to join in on the group's laughter. Instead, tell Jamie that it's not okay that he took the video of Erika and it's not okay to share the video with others, especially on social media. Encourage Jamie to delete the video from his phone, apologize to Erika, and commit to not posting or sharing the video any further. You can also offer to go with Jamie for support when he talks to Erika. If Jamie doesn't listen, telling a trusted adult what happened may be the next best option, so they can intervene and guide the next steps.

SCENARIO 2

Two of your friends are arguing by text and they're forwarding each other's messages to you, including mean comments, hoping to get you to pick a side. You feel torn. *What do you do? How could you be a good friend?*

Consider the facts: Though these are your friends, it's not your responsibility to solve their arguments. It is also okay to decide you don't want to be put in the middle of their conflict.

Ways to be a good friend: Let each friend know that you care about them both and you don't want to get involved in hurting either of them. Set a boundary by telling them you aren't going to pick a side. Encourage them to talk to each other after they have taken a break to think about the situation. Suggest that they talk with each other on the phone or in person, without making mean comments, so they can try to come to an understanding as friends. By being clear with and supportive to them both, you are modeling how to be a good friend.

SCENARIO 3

While sitting in the school cafeteria, you notice your classmate Alisha, who usually sits quietly by herself. She is being picked on by Amy, another classmate who thinks she's all that. *What do you do? How could you be a good friend?*

Consider the facts: Bullying is never okay. It causes harm to everyone involved—the person being bullied, the person practicing the toxic and unhealthy bullying behaviors, and anyone witnessing the harm. The best way to end bullying is clearly telling the person doing the bullying that the behavior will not be tolerated.

Ways to be a good friend: Tell Amy that what she's doing isn't cool, which will help Alisha feel supported and will show anyone else watching that bullying another person is not okay. Since there is strength in numbers, you could also ask a friend to come with you when you speak to Amy. People who bully often stop when they know many others disagree with their behavior. You could also let a teacher or adult in the cafeteria know this is going on, so they can take the appropriate steps to keep the space safe from bullying.

Knowing how to handle tough situations in friendships and social interactions during puberty takes practice and support. If you ever feel challenged by a situation, talk with someone you trust who can help you think through the best approach and guide you along the path to being a good friend.

More Than Friends?

Have you ever found yourself daydreaming about someone? Maybe you feel butterflies in your stomach when you're around a certain person, or you feel an overwhelming desire to be close to them. You might even want to have them be your boyfriend, girlfriend, or themfriend.

This is a common experience for tweens and teens, and it's usually called having a crush. Crushes are those "more than friends" feelings, infatuations, or romantic attractions toward another person. Like so many aspects of puberty, crushes are the result of hormonal changes, which can cause both pleasant and complicated feelings. These shifts could have you feeling drawn to someone in a new way based on certain qualities, like their personality, physical traits, talents, sense of humor, or something else unique to them.

—— FUN FACT ——

Being near your crush can cause physical changes in the body, like the release of hormones in the brain called epinephrine and norepinephrine. This release can make your heart temporarily beat faster when you're around your crush.

Attraction can be complicated to explain or understand, even when you're the one experiencing it—and that's okay! Try to observe your feelings without inviting shame to the party. Society often assumes that all kids are cisgender, and that only boys like girls and that only girls crush on boys. These are harmful assumptions that can create the sense of having to "come out" if your feelings are not within this limited binary. It shouldn't be this way. The truth is, people can feel attracted to others of the same gender or of a different gender. People can also not feel attraction to anyone, of any gender, and that's totally okay, too.

A person's identity related to the gender or genders they are or are not attracted to is called **sexual orientation**, and there are many ways people can identify. To learn more about identity terms, check out the Glossary of Terms starting on page 156. When it comes to identity terms, remember that people get to define their own identity and experiences, and that it's important to be respectful of what people share about themselves. At the same time, there is no rush to figure out which identity labels apply to you, especially while you're still growing up. Even though these terms exist, no one should ever be forced to define themselves to others.

When it comes to crushes during puberty, most of all I hope you'll think about them as valuable learning experiences, without any pressure to have a specific outcome. Crushes provide opportunities to explore and understand emotions, identities, likes, dislikes, and desires. They can also contribute to the development of important social and communication skills. It's also totally okay if you don't feel interested in crushes or romantic relationships during puberty. No matter what, remember to keep communication open with your trusted adult or someone you feel safe turning to. Relationships and crushes can spark a mix of feelings and sometimes new dilemmas to navigate, so it's helpful to have support.

Let's Write About It!

This section is just for your thoughts! Grab your notebook, paper, or device, and remember, there are no wrong answers.

* Think of someone in your life who has been a good friend or support to you. Write about what makes them a good friend.
* Now write about the ways you show you are a good friend to them.
* Make a list of the top five qualities you look for in a friend or crush.

Let's Talk About It!

With a parent, trusted adult, or friend, read these questions out loud and start chatting together.

* Have you ever witnessed or experienced an unhealthy friendship or bullying? How did it make you feel? What did you do?
* To ask a trusted adult: Think back to a significant friendship, crush, or relationship you had growing up. What made it feel healthy or unhealthy?

Let's Have Fun with It!

Take the learning into your world by trying out this activity.

Think of one thing you can say to or do for your good friend that you wrote about above to let them know how much you appreciate their support. For example: sending them thanks by text, writing them a thoughtful card, or bringing their favorite snack to them.

The End . . .
or Just the Beginning?

Congratulations! You've made it to the very end of this book! You've learned so much!

The journey doesn't end here, of course. In many ways, it's only beginning! Stay curious. Keep learning and talking with trusted friends and family, so you have support along the way. I know puberty can feel awkward sometimes, but it's all a part of the process of *growing into you*! I hope this book continues to be a trusted resource that you can return to as your body changes. I hope it reminds you that you deserve to understand and care for your body without shame or taboo.

Let's Write About It!

This section is just for your thoughts! Grab your notebook, paper, or device, and remember, there are no wrong answers.

* Let's time-travel into the future, about 15 years from now, and imagine your adult self. Write a letter to your future self, sharing what you hope you will be doing to live your best life.
* Include in your letter any goals, activities, self-care rituals, and parts of your identity you hope you'll grow into as this future self.
* Draw a picture or create a collage of images or words that represents what you hope for in your future. Anything is possible, so try not to limit your daydreaming.

Let's Talk About It!

With a parent, trusted adult, or friend, read these questions out loud and start chatting together.

* This book shared a lot of knowledge about bodies and puberty! What information did you find most interesting? What are you curious to learn more about?
* To ask a trusted adult: What values or experiences do you hope for me and my puberty journey?

Let's Have Fun with It!

Take the learning into your world by trying out this activity.

Make a time capsule to remind your future self of the you that you are today. Choose a few items that are a part of your life, interests, or identity now. These could include a picture of yourself, your family, your best friend, or your crush; an outfit, team jersey, or accessory; art you've created; a favorite toy; an old phone; or something memorable from your school year. These items should have some meaning or sentimental value to you.

Get a shoe box, jar, or container big enough to hold the items. Then add your items to it and store your time capsule in a safe place where you can easily find it in the future, like in a closet or under your bed. Make a plan to open it once you graduate from high school, to see how far you've come and to give yourself a sweet blast from the past.

Trusted Resources to Continue the Learning

There's always more to learn, and I want to leave you with resources to help you stay curious, learn, and connect. Here is a list of trusted, inclusive resources that can help you, and your family, dig deeper into the many topics discussed in this book as you're *growing into you*!

BOOKS FOR TWEENS AND YOUNG TEENS

This Period in My Life: A Period Guide Book and Journal by Saskia Boujo (Saskia Boujo, 2020)

Roads to Family: All the Ways We Come to Be by Rachel H. S. Ginocchio (Twenty-First Century Books, 2023)

Vaginas and Periods 101: A Pop-Up Book by Christian Hoeger and Kristen Lilla (Sex Ed Talk, LLC, 2019)

The P Word: A Manual for Mammals by David Hu (Science, Naturally!, 2023)

First Phone: A Child's Guide to Digital Responsibility, Safety, and Etiquette by Catherine Pearlman (TarcherPerigee, 2022)

The Every Body Book: The LGBTQ+ Inclusive Guide for Kids About Sex, Gender, Bodies, and Families by Rachel E. Simon (Jessica Kingsley Publishers, 2020)

The Every Body Book of Consent: An LGBTQIA-Inclusive Guide to Respecting Boundaries, Bodies, and Beyond by Rachel E. Simon (Jessica Kingsley Publishers, 2024)

Sex Is a Funny Word: A Book About Bodies, Feelings, and You by Cory Silverberg and Fiona Smyth (Triangle Square, 2015)

You Know, Sex: Bodies, Gender, Puberty, and Other Things by Cory Silverberg and Fiona Smyth (Triangle Square, 2022)

The Autism-Friendly Guide to Periods by Robyn Steward (Jessica Kingsley Publishers, 2019)

The Book of Radical Answers: Real Questions from Real Kids Just Like You by Sonya Renee Taylor (Dial Books, 2023)

Celebrate Your Body (and Its Changes, Too!): The Ultimate Puberty Book for Girls by Sonya Renee Taylor (Callisto Kids, 2018)

Growing Up Great!: The Ultimate Puberty Book for Boys by Scott Todnem (Callisto Kids, 2019)

Beyond the Gender Binary by Alok Vaid-Menon (Penguin Workshop, 2020)

WEBSITES AND ORGANIZATIONS

AMAZE, amaze.org Offers engaging, inclusive animated videos and digital resources for tweens, teens, and families about bodies, puberty, gender, relationships, consent, and sex

Every Body Curious, everybodycurious.com Offers fun, inclusive videos for tweens and teens about bodies, puberty, gender, relationships, consent, and more

Gender Spectrum, genderspectrum.org Offers a comprehensive collection of resources, guides, and support to help young people, parents, and caring adults learn about gender diversity

Growing Into You!™: Puberty Education for Families, giypuberty.com Offers interactive, gender-inclusive, fully virtual puberty and sex education for 8- to 15-year-olds and their trusted adults

Healthy Children, healthychildren.org Offers medically accurate information and resources, from the American Academy of Pediatrics, on child development from birth through the teen years

interACT, interactadvocates.org Advocates for and offers education and resources in support of the human rights of people born with intersex traits

InterConnect, interconnect.support A community providing connection, support, and education for intersex individuals, their family members, and allies

Intersex Justice Project, intersexjusticeproject.org An advocacy organization that works to end invasive and unnecessary surgeries on intersex youth by empowering intersex people of color as changemakers

PFLAG, pflag.org A national organization that provides education, support, and advocacy for LGBTQ+ people and their families

Roo by Planned Parenthood, roo.plannedparenthood.org A free 24/7 chatbot that provides medically accurate, inclusive answers to young people's questions about bodies, puberty, gender, relationships, and sexual health

The Trevor Project, thetrevorproject.org Offers crisis intervention, resources, and supportive services for LGBTQ+ youth and their families, including a crisis hotline at 1-866-488-7386 and text support (text "START" to 678-678)

Trans Lifeline, translifeline.org A trans-led organization that offers a peer support hotline at 1-877-565-8860 and resources for trans and nonbinary people

RESOURCES FOR PARENTS AND CARING ADULTS

Sex Positive Talks to Have with Kids: A Guide to Raising Sexually Healthy, Informed, Empowered Young People by Melissa Pintor Carnagey (Self-published, 2020)

The Gender Identity Guide for Parents: Compassionate Advice to Help Your Child Be Their Most Authentic Self by Tavi Hawn (Callisto, 2022)

This Is So Awkward: Modern Puberty Explained by Cara Natterson and Vanessa Kroll Bennett (Rodale Books, 2023)

BLOOM, **bloomforall.com** Offers medically accurate, inclusive information and resources to support young people and parents through puberty and the teen years

You can find more great resources to support your puberty journey by visiting giypuberty.com/book/resources. Or scan the QR code.

Glossary of Terms

Definitions can provide helpful information and context as you're learning about bodies, puberty, gender, and sexual health. When it comes to identity terms, remember that people get to define their own identity and experiences, and no one should ever be forced to define or label themselves to others. It's also important to note that language is always changing and can be a tool with the power to both uplift and affirm as well as stigmatize or harm. Be mindful of the ways you use language. Stay open to learning from others and from the ever-evolving world around you.

Acne: Also called pimples or zits, this is a skin condition that occurs when pores become clogged or inflamed with oil and dead skin cells.

Adam's apple: The cartilage that covers the front of the larynx and is a visible bump on the front of some people's throats.

Agender (or genderless): Describes someone who does not identify with a gender. Some agender people use the term *gender neutral* or *neutrois*, some define their gender as unknown or not definable, and some do not think of gender as a way to define themselves.

Anus: The opening between the buttocks where feces (poop) and gas (farts) exit the body.

Aromantic: Describes someone who experiences little to no romantic attraction.

Asexual (or ace/aces): Describes someone who experiences little or no sexual attraction, or who experiences attraction but doesn't feel the need to act out that attraction sexually. They may still date and have fulfilling relationships. Asexual people can also identify in many other ways.

Bigender: Describes someone who identifies with two genders.

Binder: A gender-affirming garment that compresses the chest area to help it appear flatter.

Bisexuality: Sexual or romantic attraction toward two or more genders.

Bladder: An internal organ where urine develops.

Boundaries: Rules you get to decide that help you feel safe and respected within interactions and relationships with others. Boundaries can be physical, emotional, and even digital.

Breasts: Mammary glands located in the chest area that are made up of fat, tissue, nerves, and milk-producing glands.

Cervical mucus: Natural fluids created by the cervix each month.

Cervix: The lower, narrow part of the uterus that connects to the vagina.

Cesarean section (or C-section): A surgical procedure in which a medical professional makes an incision wide enough and deep enough in the abdomen of a pregnant person, in order to reach inside the uterus and remove the baby.

Chosen name: A name that transgender, nonbinary, and/or gender-diverse people choose for themselves that aligns with who they are more than the name they were given at birth. Using a person's chosen name is an important way to respect and affirm them.

Chromosome: A threadlike structure made of protein and DNA that is found in the nucleus of most living cells and carries genetic information.

Circumcision: A surgical procedure, typically conducted within the first week of a newborn's life, in which the foreskin of the penis is removed.

Cisgender (or cis): Describes a person who is the gender they were assigned at birth based on assumptions about the body parts they have.

Cisheteronormativity: A worldview that elevates heterosexuality, the gender binary, and social norms related to heterosexuality as normal, preferred, or the default. Cisheteronormativity assumes that all people are either cis boys/men or cis girls/women, and that everyone is heterosexual. The influence of cisheteronormative views can be found in many aspects of a culture, such as books, movies, sports, language, science, bathrooms, etc.

Clitoris: An organ located in the vulva area that is made of erectile tissue and is packed with thousands of nerve ends that play a role in pleasure. The tip of the clitoris is called the *glans*.

Consent: An agreement between people that involves communication—verbal or nonverbal—and respect, should be freely given, and is retractable without coercion or force.

Cortisol: A hormone that helps regulate the stress response, metabolism, immune system, blood pressure, and sleep patterns.

Cowper's gland: A gland that produces pre-ejaculate fluid.

Deadname: The legal name that a transgender, nonbinary, and/or gender-diverse person was given by their parents or caregivers when they were born that the person no longer uses. *Deadnaming* is a form of misgendering by saying or writing someone's deadname without their consent. This can be very harmful, distressing, and sometimes even unsafe, as it can "out" people without their permission. Use people's accurate names, not deadnames, even when you refer to them from before they chose their new name.

Demisexual: Describes someone who only experiences sexual attraction once they form an emotional connection with someone else.

Dopamine: A neurotransmitter that helps regulate movements, memory, moods, sleep, motivation, and the ability to feel pleasure.

Ejaculation: When sperm, semen, or vaginal fluids exit the body.

Emotional attraction: A feeling of deep connection to another person, with or without physical elements of attraction.

Endometriosis: A condition in which tissue that's similar to uterine lining grows in areas outside the uterus, which can cause increased menstrual pain, abnormal vaginal bleeding, and chronic pain in the lower back and pelvis.

Endorphins: Neurotransmitters that help relieve pain, reduce stress, and regulate mood. They can be released during activities like running, dancing, swimming, eating, and sex.

Epididymis: A duct-like organ connected to the testes where sperm mature before traveling through the vas deferens.

Erection: When a penis temporarily hardens and becomes firm.

Estrogen: A hormone produced in the ovaries, testes, adrenal glands, and adipose tissue that plays a role in sexual and reproductive development, bone health, muscle growth, memory, and overall health.

Fallopian tubes: The passages through which the ova (eggs) travel to the uterus.

Flaccid: Describes a penis that is soft, hanging loosely, and not erect.

Follicular phase: The second phase of the menstrual cycle when the ova (eggs) in the ovaries are preparing for release.

Foreskin: A retractable fold of skin that covers the shaft and glans of the penis.

Free bleeding: Menstruating without using period care products to manage the flow.

Gender-affirming care: Life-saving healthcare for transgender, nonbinary, and gender-diverse people that affirm their gender identity. Examples include hormone therapies and gender-affirming surgeries.

Gender and sexuality alliance (GSA) or queer student alliance (QSA): School-based groups that provide safe and affirming spaces for queer students. They often plan events and help make schools more inclusive.

Gender binary: The belief that gender identity has only two distinct, opposite, and disconnected forms (boys/men and girls/women) and that there are only two types of bodies (male and female) that define gender experience. A binary view of gender and bodies assumes that if you have a penis you must be a boy, and if you have a vulva you must be a girl. This myth excludes many people, ignores the vastness of gender, and is one part of transphobia.

Gender dysphoria: A state of intense distress caused by feeling misalignment with the gender you were assigned at birth. Not all transgender, nonbinary, and/or gender-diverse people experience gender dysphoria.

Gender euphoria: A state of feeling joy and alignment with your gender.

Gender expression: The physical representation of a person's gender through things like their clothing choices, hair, or personal style. Through a binary lens, it can relate to how feminine or masculine a person presents, but it can be a mix or neither of these. Examples of terms related to gender expression are *feminine, masculine, androgynous, neutral, conforming,* and *nonconforming*. Any gender can have any gender expression, and a person's gender expression does not determine the pronouns they use.

Genderfluid: Describes someone whose gender identity and/or expression varies and is not attached to one gender. Genderfluid people experience gender in a unique way that changes over time and/or does not always fit into boxes.

Gender identity: How someone is or knows themselves to be relative to gender. Some examples are *girl/woman, boy/man, femme, transgender, nonbinary, genderfluid, genderqueer*. Each person's gender is as unique as stars in the universe!

Gender nonconforming: Describes someone whose gender identity and/or gender expression does not conform to the cultural or social expectations of gender. This can be an umbrella term for many identities including, but not limited to, genderfluid, gender expansive, and gender nonbinary. Gender nonconformity can also be a part of being cisgender, if you don't follow binary stereotypes or societal expectations, for example, if you are a girl who has a buzz cut or a boy who wears a dress.

Gender norms: Constructed "rules" or ideas about the way members of certain genders "should" look and behave.

Genderqueer: Describes someone whose gender identity and/or expression falls between, outside of, or within the gender binary.

Homologous: Describes two different body parts that have similar features, such as the glans clitoris and the penis.

Hormones: Chemicals in the body that act like messengers, carrying signals for the body to change, regulate, balance, and/or grow.

Hygiene: Habits and routines of grooming and taking care of the body.

Hypothalamus: A part of the brain that produces hormones and plays a significant role in starting puberty.

In vitro fertilization (IVF): A medical procedure that brings an ovum and sperm together in a laboratory. After they are successfully joined, the fertilized ovum, or embryo, is placed into a uterus to continue developing. This method is one way queer families and/or people who cannot otherwise become pregnant can create babies.

Intersex: Describes a person that is born with genitals, chromosome patterns, internal organs, or hormone levels that fall outside of what's typically categorized as female or male. Because of these varying factors that aren't always visible at birth, a person may not learn they are intersex until puberty or later in life, or they may never find this out about themselves.

Intrauterine insemination (IUI): A procedure that places sperm directly inside a uterus to allow for reproduction.

Labia: The inner and outer folds of skin located on the vulva. The inner labia are also called the *labia minora*. The outer labia are also called the *labia majora*.

Larynx: A hollow muscular organ that acts as a passageway for air to the lungs and that contains the vocal cords.

LGBTQIA2S+: An acronym that commonly stands for *lesbian*, *gay*, *bisexual*, *transgender*, *queer* or *questioning*, *intersex*, *asexual* or *agender*, and *Two-Spirit*. The plus sign represents the vastness of many more identities and orientations.

Luteal phase: The last phase of the menstrual cycle, when the ovum lands inside the uterus and either dissolves, if not fertilized by sperm, or begins to develop a fetus, if fertilized.

Masturbation: Touching your own body for pleasure.

Menarche: A person's first period.

Menstrual phase: One of four phases of the menstrual cycle, considered the start, when the period bleeding occurs.

Menstruation (or period): The shedding from the uterus of the thick endometrial lining that develops during ovulation.

Misgendering: Using language toward or to describe a transgender, nonbinary, genderqueer, agender, and/or gender-diverse person that doesn't align with their affirmed gender. Misgendering can happen by not using a person's pronouns, using gendering language that doesn't match the person, or using a person's deadname. Misgendering is harmful, even if it's not done on purpose, and it's important to learn about and use language that affirms others.

Misogyny: Hatred, prejudice, or discrimination against women or girls that is rooted in the belief that women or girls are inferior to men or boys.

Neurotransmitters: Chemical messengers in the body that carry signals from one nerve cell to the next and are responsible for many functions of the body like movement, sensations, and heartbeats.

Nocturnal emission (or wet dream): Ejaculation that happens while a person is sleeping.

Nonbinary: Describes a person who is not a boy or girl, but instead somewhere in the gender universe rather than the gender binary. Since babies are not (yet!) assigned nonbinary at birth, nonbinary people can be transgender. Some nonbinary people also use the word *genderqueer* to describe themselves.

Ova (singular: ovum): The cells located in the ovaries of a person with a uterus, which contain half of what is needed genetically to create new life.

Ovaries: Two almond-shaped organs in the body of a person with a uterus where the ova are stored.

Ovulatory phase: The third phase of the menstrual cycle, when one ovum is released and begins to travel through the fallopian tube toward the uterus.

Oxytocin: A hormone that plays a big role in many human and social behaviors like feeling trust, bonding, and forming romantic attachment to others. It also plays a part in causing contractions needed during childbirth, breastfeeding, and ejaculation.

Packer: Gender-affirming padding or a penis-shaped object worn in the underwear to create the appearance of a penis or bulge.

Pangender: Describes someone whose identity consists of all or many gender identities and expressions.

Pansexual: Describes someone who experiences emotional, romantic, or sexual attraction to people of any gender, or someone who does not consider gender as a factor when being attracted to another person.

Penis: An external organ made of erectile tissue that consists of two parts—the shaft and the glans (the tip, sometimes called the *head*)—and can transfer urine, sperm, and semen.

Period poverty: The inaccessibility of menstrual care products and education about periods.

Period tax (or tampon tax): Unfair laws that add sales tax to the cost of period care products bought in stores, instead of treating period care products as nontaxable items like other basic necessities.

Physical attraction: A part of sexual identity often representing a draw or desire toward another person in a sexual or physical way.

Pituitary gland: A pea-sized gland located at the base of the brain that plays a significant role in starting puberty.

Pleasure: An experience or feeling of satisfaction or enjoyment.

Pornography (or porn): Images, video, audio, or text that uses naked bodies or sexual acts for adult entertainment or to make money.

Premenstrual dysphoric disorder (PMDD): A condition that happens during the luteal phase of the menstrual cycle, causing severe symptoms of depression, irritability, anxiety, and tension.

Premenstrual syndrome (PMS): A group of physical and emotional symptoms—including mood swings, tender breasts, food cravings, fatigue, and irritability—that result from hormone shifts one to two weeks before the menstrual phase of the cycle.

Progesterone: A hormone that supports menstruation by thickening the uterine lining to prepare it for a fertilized egg. Progesterone also plays a part in emotional regulation, testosterone production, and balancing estrogen.

Pronouns: Words that refer to who a person is talking to or talking about. For example: she/her/hers/herself; they/them/theirs/themself; ze/zir/zirs/zirself; and he/him/his/himself. A person determines which pronouns they use, and these do not always correlate with the person's gender. Using someone's correct pronouns is a basic way to show someone respect. Pronouns are not "preferred"; they are what is most true. Saying "preferred" when speaking of someone's pronouns can imply they are optional.

Pronouns Chart*			
Subjective	Objective	Possessive	Reflexive
She	Her	Hers	Herself
He	Him	His	Himself
They	Them	Theirs	Themself
Ze (pronounced "zee")	Zir (pronounced "zeer")	Zirs	Zirself

*These are just a few of many pronoun options.

Prostate gland: A gland that produces seminal fluid.

Puberty: A process of changes that causes a child's body to mature into an adult body. This maturing develops the brain, bones, emotions, and even the ability to reproduce.

Puberty blockers: Medications prescribed by an endocrinologist that pause puberty from happening by blocking the release of certain hormones. Puberty blockers can give trans, nonbinary, and/or gender-diverse young people who are experiencing gender dysphoria time to figure out which puberty changes most align with who they are. Puberty blockers are a part of lifesaving care for a young person and are prescribed in collaboration with medical providers and primary caregivers.

Queer: A term used to express the vastness of identities and orientations. In the past, *queer* was a negative or derogatory term for people who are gay, and thus it is sometimes disliked. The term is increasingly being used to describe all identities and politics that go against normative beliefs. The term is valued by many LGBTQIA2S+ people for its defiance and sense of community.

Rape (related terms: sexual assault, sexual abuse): Nonconsensual sexual activity that is a crime.

Reproduction (to reproduce): The process of creating new life, which happens when an ovum is fertilized by sperm. For humans, this can happen through some types of sex or with the help of medical interventions.

Scrotum: The sack of skin that contains and protects the testicles.

Sebum: An oily secretion of the pores.

Self-care: Practices that nourish your own mind, body, and spirit.

Glossary of Terms

Self-compassion: Treating yourself with kindness and acceptance, especially when you make mistakes or are feeling unsure of yourself.

Semen: The whitish fluid that's produced in the seminal vesicles and prostate gland.

Seminal vesicles: Two glands that produce semen.

Serotonin: A neurotransmitter that helps regulate sleep, moods, and healing of wounds.

Sex: A consensual activity that adults, and some older teens who feel ready, can do. Sometimes just for pleasure, to build intimacy, and/or to make babies. There are many ways people can have sex.

Sex assigned at birth (or biological sex): A label that was created by people over time to reinforce the myth that there are only two types of bodies. Sex assignments are often given when a person is born and are based on an assessment of their external genitals. Examples of these terms are *female* (often assigned to babies who have a vulva), *male* (often assigned to babies who have a penis), and *intersex* (often assigned to babies for whom there is a noticeable variation to the external genitals).

Sex positive: An open, affirming, and judgment-free attitude toward human sexuality and sex that regards all consensual experiences as fundamentally healthy.

Sexual health: A state of physical, emotional, mental, spiritual, and social well-being as it relates to sexuality.

Sperm: The cell produced in the testicles that contains half of what is needed genetically to create new life.

Stand-to-pee (STP): A gender-affirming device that allows people with vulvas to pee while standing. Some are in the shape of a penis, while others are funnel-shaped. STPs can help people use a bathroom that aligns with their gender and/or can help gender-diverse people feel gender euphoria.

Stereotype: A mistaken belief about a particular group of people, which can lead to harmful or limiting assumptions about all people in that group.

Supernumerary nipples: A condition of having more than two nipples on the body.

Terminal hair: The thicker, longer, and often darker hair that grows on certain parts of the body.

Testicles (or testes): Oval-shaped organs that produce sperm and hormones such as testosterone, estrogen, and progesterone.

Testosterone: A hormone produced in the ovaries and testes that plays a role in sexual and reproductive development, bone health, sleep, cognition, and overall health.

Toxic masculinity: A harmful perception of manliness that encourages men and boys to be dominant and aggressive and to suppress emotions.

Transition: A term sometimes used to refer to the social, legal, and/or medical process some transgender, nonbinary, genderqueer, and other gender-diverse people go through to discover and/or affirm their gender identity. This may, but does not always, include taking hormones; having gender affirming surgeries; changing clothing or hair styles; sharing one's identity with friends and family; and changing names, pronouns, and identification documents. Many individuals choose not to or are unable to transition for a wide range of reasons both within and beyond their control. A person does not have to experience such transitions in order to identify as transgender, nonbinary, genderqueer, or gender diverse.

Transgender (or trans): Describes a person whose gender is different from the gender they were assigned at birth. Trans people are misgendered at birth based on assumptions about body parts.

Transphobia: Negative beliefs about what it means to be transgender, nonbinary, and gender nonconforming. These beliefs harm and erase transgender, nonbinary, and gender-diverse people and their experiences. Transphobia affects the way people, the government, media, and societal systems generally treat people whose identities do not fit into typical gender roles.

Trusted adult: A grown-up that is chosen by a young person as a safe, nonjudgmental, and supportive figure in their life.

Two-Spirit: A term proposed and coined by Myra Laramee during the Third Annual Intertribal Native American, First Nations, Gay and Lesbian American Conference held in Winnipeg, to describe Native people who fulfill a traditional third-gender, or gender-variant, social role in their communities.

Urethral opening: A hole located above the vaginal opening and at the tip of the penis where urine (pee) exits the body.

Uterine fibroids: Noncancerous growths that occur inside or around the uterus. They can vary in size and can change the shape of the uterus. Symptoms of uterine fibroids can include heavy or long menstrual periods, pelvic pain, urinary or bowel issues, and pain in the back and/or legs.

Uterine lining (or endometrium): Connective tissue that develops inside the uterus throughout each month.

Uterus: The internal organ, about the size of a pear, in which endometrial lining can develop during menstrual cycles and where a fertilized ovum can develop into a fetus.

Vagina: The internal muscular tube of about 3 to 5 inches in length that leads from the cervix to the outside of the body.

Vaginal discharge: Natural fluids created within the vagina that exit the body through the vaginal opening.

Values: A person's principles or standards of behavior; one's judgment of what is important in their life.

Vas deferens: The tube that carries sperm from the testes to the urethra.

Vellus hair (or peach fuzz): The thin, shorter, often lighter-colored hair that grows all over the body.

Vulva: External genitalia that includes parts such as the mons pubis, inner and outer labia, glans clitoris, urethral opening, and vaginal opening.

For a more expansive glossary of gender and sexual identity terms, check out the resources available through sites like hrc.org and plannedparenthood.org.

References

ABOUT THE AUTHOR (THAT'S ME!)

Carnagey, Melissa P. 2020. *Sex Positive Talks to Have with Kids: A Guide to Raising Sexually Healthy, Informed, Empowered Young People*. Self-published.

"Are You an Askable Parent?" Advocates for Youth. https://www.advocatesforyouth.org/resources/health-information/are-you-an-askable-parent.

PUBERTY IS NOT . . .

"Dog Puberty." Purina. https://www.purina.co.uk/articles/dogs/puppy/health/dog-puberty.

"Do Cats Go Through Puberty?" Cats.com. https://cats.com/do-cats-go-through-puberty.

PUBERTY STARTS HERE!

"What Is Intersex?" interACT. https://interactadvocates.org/faq.

"Serotonin." Cleveland Clinic. https://my.clevelandclinic.org/health/articles/22572-serotonin.

"Dopamine." Cleveland Clinic. https://my.clevelandclinic.org/health/articles/22581-dopamine.

"Oxytocin." Cleveland Clinic. https://my.clevelandclinic.org/health/articles/22618-oxytocin.

"Endorphins." Cleveland Clinic. https://my.clevelandclinic.org/health/body/23040-endorphins.

"Cortisol." Cleveland Clinic. https://my.clevelandclinic.org/health/articles/22187-cortisol.

ALL ABOUT ANATOMY: WHAT'S UP DOWN THERE?

"Male Reproductive System." Nemours TeensHealth. https://kidshealth.org/en/teens/male-repro.html.

"Female Reproductive System." Nemours TeensHealth. https://kidshealth.org/en/teens/female-repro.html.

"Puberty." Planned Parenthood. https://www.plannedparenthood.org/learn/teens/puberty.

"What Does Intersex Look Like?" interACT. https://interactadvocates.org/faq/#look-like.

SIGNS OF PUBERTY

Natterson, Cara MD, and Vanessa Kroll Bennett. 2023. *This Is So Awkward: Modern Puberty Explained*. Rodale Books.

"What Is Vellus Hair?" Healthline. https://www.healthline.com/health/vellus-hair.

"Third Nipple." Cleveland Clinic. https://my.clevelandclinic.org/health/

diseases/25167-third-nipple.

"What's Your Nipple Type? And 24 Other Nipple Facts." Healthline. https://www.healthline.com/health/nipple-facts-male-and-female#4.-Inverted-nipples-are-normal.

"Physical Changes During Puberty." Healthy Children by the American Academy of Pediatrics. https://www.healthychildren.org/English/ages-stages/gradeschool/puberty/Pages/Physical-Development-of-School-Age-Children.aspx.

"Why Is My Voice Changing?" Nemours KidsHealth. https://kidshealth.org/en/teens/voice-changing.html.

PUBERTY ACROSS THE GENDER UNIVERSE

"A Map of Gender-Diverse Cultures." PBS. https://www.pbs.org/independentlens/content/two-spirits_map-html.

"6 Cultures That Recognize More than Two Genders." Britannica. https://www.britannica.com/list/6-cultures-that-recognize-more-than-two-genders.

"Trans Summer School: Gender Expression Gear." Scarleteen. https://www.scarleteen.com/trans_summer_school_gender_expression_gear.

Erickson-Schroth, Laura, ed. 2022. *Trans Bodies, Trans Selves: A Resource by and for Transgender Communities*. 2nd ed. Oxford University Press.

Finley, L. C. 2024. *Health Ed for Every Kid Learning Unit*. Self-published.

Gonzales, Kathryn MBA, and Karen Rayne PhD. 2019. *Trans+: Love, Sex, Romance, and Being You*. Magination Press.

"Get the Facts on Gender-Affirming Care." Human Rights Campaign. https://www.hrc.org/resources/get-the-facts-on-gender-affirming-care.

ABOUT BODY IMAGE

"Body Image: Pre-Teens and Teenagers." Raisingchildren.net.au. https://raisingchildren.net.au/pre-teens/healthy-lifestyle/body-image/body-image-teens.

Natterson, Cara MD, and Vanessa Kroll Bennett. 2023. *This Is So Awkward: Modern Puberty Explained*. Rodale Books.

HYGIENE HACKS

"What Can I Do About Acne?" Nemours TeensHealth. https://kidshealth.org/en/teens/prevent-acne.html.

"Teen Acne: How to Treat and Prevent This Common Skin Condition." Healthy Children by the American Academy of Pediatrics. https://www.healthychildren.org/English/health-issues/conditions/skin/Pages/What-Causes-Acne.aspx.

"Does Drinking Water Help Acne?" Healthline. https://www.healthline.com/nutrition/does-drinking-water-help-acne.

"Hygiene Basics." Nemours TeensHealth. https://kidshealth.org/en/teens/hygiene-basics.html.

Natterson, Cara MD, and Vanessa Kroll Bennett. 2023. *This Is So Awkward: Modern Puberty Explained*. Rodale Books.

PERIOD POWER!

"Menarche." Cleveland Clinic. https://my.clevelandclinic.org/health/diseases/24139-menarche.

"Stages of the Menstrual Cycle." Healthline. https://www.healthline.com/health/womens-health/stages-of-menstrual-cycle.

"Uterine Fibroids and Endometriosis." Endometriosis.net. https://endometriosis.net/clinical/uterine-fibroids.

Natterson, Cara MD, and Vanessa Kroll Bennett. 2023. *This Is So Awkward: Modern Puberty Explained*. Rodale Books.

"How to Use Menstrual Hygiene Products." Planned Parenthood. https://www.plannedparenthood.org/learn/health-and-wellness/menstruation/how-to-use-menstrual-hygiene-products.

Boujo, Saskia. 2020. *This Period in My Life: A Period Guide Book and Journal*. Saskia Boujo.

"13 Things to Know About Free Bleeding." Healthline. https://www.healthline.com/health/free-bleeding.

"Menstrual Product Makers Form Coalition to Reimburse 'Tampon Tax' to Shoppers." CNN. https://www.cnn.com/2023/10/11/business/period-products-makers-coalition-tampon-tax/index.html.

PLANNING FOR SELF-CARE

"Healthy Food for Pre-Teens and Teenagers: the 5 Food Groups." Raisingchildren.net.au. https://raisingchildren.net.au/teens/healthy-lifestyle/daily-food-guides/nutrition-healthy-food-teens.

EXPLORING PLEASURE

"Masturbation." Healthy Children by the American Academy of Pediatrics. https://www.healthychildren.org/English/ages-stages/gradeschool/puberty/Pages/Masturbation.aspx.

PRACTICING CONSENT AND BOUNDARIES

"All About Consent." Kids Helpline. https://kidshelpline.com.au/teens/issues/what-consent.

GLOSSARY OF TERMS

Carnagey, Melissa P. 2020. *Sex Positive Talks to Have with Kids: A Guide to Raising Sexually Healthy, Informed, Empowered Young People*. Self-published.

Cleveland Clinic. https://my.clevelandclinic.org.

Finley, L. C. 2024. *Health Ed for Every Kid Learning Unit*. Self-published.

"Glossary of Terms." Human Rights Campaign. https://www.hrc.org/resources/glossary-of-terms.

Index

A

acne, 58, 87–88, 156
Adam's apples, 60–61, 156
adults, trusted, 14–15
affirmations, 25
agender (genderless), 29, 156
amaze.org, 81
anatomy, 37–53; intersex traits, 48–49; penis, scrotum, testicles, etc., 44–49; terms for, 37; vulva, vagina, uterus, etc., 38–43. See also body
andropause, 32
animals, puberty in, 22
anus, 40, 48, 92, 156
arguments, between friends, 144–45
aromantic, 156
asexual (ace / aces), 72, 156
attraction to others, 147–49; emotional, 157; physical, 160

B

bigender, 156
binary, 21, 66, 158. See also gender / gender identity; transgender / trans
binders, 69, 156
biological sex, 29–30, 162
bisexuality, 72, 156
bladder, 39, 156
BO (body odor), 61–62, 89

body: changes in, 27–36, 37, 54–64; consent and boundaries for, 135–41; nourishing and moving, 59–60. See also anatomy; hygiene
body hair, 54–56; changing, 39, 55–56, 89–91; pubic hair, 39, 44, 48; types of, 54, 162, 163
body image, 80–86
body odor (BO), 61–62, 89
boobs. See breasts
boundaries, 135–41, 156
brain, changes in, 28–32
bras, 57, 69
breast buds, 56
breasts, 56–57, 156. See also bras
bullying, 145–46
butthole. See anus

C

celebrating yourself, 83–84
cervical mucus, 41, 92, 156
cervix, 42, 156
Chalmers, Leona, 119
childbirth, 40, 41
chosen name, 156–57
chromosome, 48, 157
circumcision, 45, 157
cisgender (cis), 147, 157
cisheteronormativity, 157

clitoris, 38, 39–40, 157

clothing, and gender expression, 68–69

coming out, 74–76, 147–48

community, 72

comparing yourself to others, 23

consent, 50, 135–41, 144, 157

cortisol, 31, 157

Cowper's gland, 47, 157

cramping, 97–98

crushes, 147–49

C-section, 41, 156

D

deadname, 157

demisexual, 157

dilbaa, 66

Diné (Navajo) people, 66

dopamine, 31, 130, 157

E

ejaculation, 39, 44, 47, 157

emotional attraction, 157

emotions, 35–36, 37. *See also* mood / mood swings

endometriosis, 98, 157

endorphins, 32, 157

epididymis, 47, 157

epinephrine, 147

erections, 44, 45, 157

estrogen, 28, 57, 157–58

exercise, 59–60, 123

F

fallopian tubes, 42, 158

femminielli, 66–67

flaccid, 45, 158

follicular phase, 158

food, 59, 124

foreskin, 45, 92, 158

free bleeding, 113–14, 158

friendship, 142–46

G

gender-affirming healthcare, 72, 112, 158

gender-affirming spaces, 72

gender and sexualities alliance (GSA), 72, 158

gender binary, 21, 66, 158. *See also* gender expression; gender / gender identity; transgender / trans

gender dysphoria, 65, 72, 110–11, 158

gender euphoria, 73, 158

gender expression, 67–68, 158. *See also* gender pronouns

genderfluid, 158

gender / gender identity, 29, 49, 65–77, 158. *See also* gender binary; gender expression; transgender / trans

gender nonconforming, 158

gender norms, 68, 77, 158–59

gender pronouns, 70–72. *See also* gender expression; gender / gender identity; transgender / trans

genderqueer, 29, 159

Gender Spectrum, 72, 75

genital hygiene, 41–42, 92

glans, 46

glans clitoris, 39

glossary, 156–63

gratitude, 124

green time, 125

growing pains, 60

growth / growth spurts, 58, 60

H

Haas, Earle, 119

hair, 54–56; changes to, 39, 55–56, 89–91; and gender expression, 70; pubic hair, 39, 44, 48; types of, 54, 162, 163

healthcare, gender-affirming, 72

height, 58

hijras, 67

Hindu society, nonbinary identity in, 67

homologous, 39, 46, 159

hormones, 28–29, 30–32; and body odor, 61–62; and breasts, 57; and crushes, 147; definition of, 159; and skin / acne, 58; and voice changes, 60

hydration, 124

hygiene, 87–94; and body odor, 62, 89; definition of, 159; genital hygiene, 41–42, 92

hypothalamus, 28, 159

I

identity terms, 148. *See also* gender / gender identity

inner labia (labia minora), 38

interACT, 49

InterConnect, 49

intersex, 48–49, 67, 159

Intersex Justice Project, 49

intrauterine insemination (IUI), 43, 159

in vitro fertilization (IVF), 43, 159

Italy, third gender in, 66–67

K

Kenner, Mary Beatrice Davidson, 119

L

labia, 38–39, 159

Laramee, Myra, 66

larynx, 60–61, 64, 159

"late bloomer," 23

LGBTQIA2S+, 72, 159

liners, 105–6

M

makeup, 69

mammary glands, 56–57

masturbation, 39, 130–34, 159

media, and body image, 80–81

menarche, 95, 159

menopause, 32

menstrual cups and discs, 108–9, 113

menstrual cycle: and acne, 88; follicular phase, 98, 158; luteal phase, 99, 159; menstrual phase, 97–98, 159; overview of, 96; ovulatory phase, 43, 99, 160; phases of, 97–100, 159, 160; regulation of, 100; and reproduction, 95. *See also* menstruation; period care; period(s) menstruation: definition of, 159; overview of, 42, 43, 95–103; period poverty, 116–17; and period underwear, 69, 106–7. *See also* menstrual cycle; period care; period(s)

misgendering, 71, 159

misogyny, 33, 159

mood / mood swings, 33–34. *See also* emotions

"morning wood," 44

N

nádleehi, 66

name, chosen, 156–57

nature, 125

Navajo (Diné) people, 66

neurotransmitters, 30, 159–60

nipples, 57, 162

nocturnal emission, 41, 44, 160

nonbinary / nonbinary identity: definition of, 160; in Hindu society, 67; and period poverty, 116; period tips for, 110–12; questions and answers on, 74–76

norepinephrine, 147

nutrition, 59, 124

O

outer labia (labia majora), 38–39

ova / ovum, 42–43, 160

ovaries, 42–43, 160

ovulation / ovulatory phase, 43, 99, 160

oxytocin, 31, 160

P

packers, 69, 160

pads, 104–5

pangender, 160

pansexual, 160

panty liners, 105–6

PCOS (polycystic ovary syndrome), 98

peeing: stand-to-pee devices, 69; and tampon use, 113

penis, 39, 44–46, 92, 160

perimenopause, 32

period care, 104–15; free bleeding, 113–14; liners, 105–6; menstrual cups and discs, 108–9, 113; overview of, 96; pads, 104–5; period kits, 110; period underwear, 69, 106–7; product selection, 114–15; products throughout history, 118–21; questions and answers on, 113–15; tampons, 107–8, 113; tips for trans, nonbinary, and gender-diverse menstruators, 110–12

Period. End of Sentence., 103

period kits, 110

period poops, 100

period poverty, 116–17, 160

period(s): definition of, 159; overview of, 43, 95–96; timing of first, 95; tracking, 100–101, 111. *See also* menstrual cycle; menstruation; period care

period tax, 116, 160

period underwear, 69, 106–7

PFLAG, 72, 75

physical attraction, 160

pimples, 58, 87–88

pituitary gland, 28, 160

playlist, 86

pleasure, 160. *See also* masturbation

PMDD (premenstrual dysphoric disorder), 98

PMS (premenstrual syndrome), 99, 160

polycystic ovary syndrome (PCOS), 98

pornography / porn, 51, 81, 160

premenstrual dysphoric disorder (PMDD), 98, 160

premenstrual syndrome (PMS), 99, 160

progesterone, 28, 57, 160

pronouns, 70–72, 161. *See also* gender expression; gender / gender identity; transgender / trans

prostate gland, 47, 161

puberty: in animals, 22; bodily changes during, 27–36, 37, 54–64; definition of, 19, 161; signs of, 54–64; timing of / in, 20, 23; what puberty is, 18–19; what puberty is not, 20–21

puberty blockers, 20, 72, 112, 161

puberty education, sex positivity in, 12–13

pubic hair, 39, 44, 48

Q

queer, 161

queer student alliance (QSA), 72, 158

questions and answers: gender identity, 74–76; moods and mood swings, 33–34; period care, 113–15; puberty, 22–23; sex, 50–51

R

rape, 51, 138, 161

reproduction, 19, 43, 95, 161

resources to continue learning, 153–55

rest, 123

restrooms, and transgender menstruators, 111

S

sanitary towels / sanitary napkins, 104–5

screen time, 123, 125

scrotum, 46, 92, 161

sebum, 58, 161

self-care, 122–27, 161

self-compassion, 124, 162

semen, 44, 47, 162

seminal vesicle, 47, 162

serotonin, 30–31, 162

sex: consent and boundaries in, 138–39; definition of, 162; questions and answers on, 50–51

sex assigned at birth, 29–30, 162

Sex Positive Families, 12

sex positive / sex positivity, 12–13, 162

sexual assault / sexual abuse, 51, 138, 161

sexual health, 162

sexual orientation, 148

shame, 9, 37, 78

shaving, 90–91

skin, 58, 87–88

smells, 61–62, 89

social media, 80–81, 125

sperm, 46, 47, 162

stand-to-pee devices (STPs), 69, 162

stereotypes, 33, 68, 162

supernumerary nipples, 57, 162

T

tampons, 107–8, 113

tampon tax, 116, 160

Tampon Tax Back Coalition, 116

Taylor, Sonya Renee, 78

terminal hair, 54, 162

testicles / testes, 46, 162

testosterone, 28, 29, 162

toxic masculinity, 33

transgender / trans, 20, 110–12, 116, 163. *See also* gender / gender identity

transition, 162–63

transphobia, 163

Trevor Project, 72, 75

trusted adults, 14–15, 163

Two-Spirit, 66, 72, 163

U

underwear, 69, 106–7

urethra / urethral opening, 39, 47, 163

urination: stand-to-pee devices (STPs), 69, 162; and tampon use, 113

uterine fibroids, 98, 163

uterine lining (endometrium), 42, 163

uterus, 42, 163

V

vaginal fluids, 41–42, 92, 163

vaginal infections, 92

vagina / vaginal opening, 38, 39, 40–42, 92, 163

Vaid-Menon, Alok, 65

values, 45, 51, 151, 163

vas deferens, 47, 163

vellus hair, 54, 163

virginity, 113

voice, deepening, 60–61, 64

vulva, 38, 92, 163

W

water, drinking, 124

weight, 58

wet dream. *See* nocturnal emission

Z

zits, 58, 87–88

Acknowledgments

This book, and all of the work that has inspired it, is absolutely a testament to the saying "If you want to go fast, go alone. If you want to go far, go together." I want to deeply thank the people and community that have been a part of my *together* for helping me, and this mission, *go far*.

To my husband, Ryan. You have been a constant, loving support, cheerleader, affirming ear, and safe space for me and for our kids. I could not have achieved all of the milestones of this work without your love as my foundation. I thank and love you so so much. xoxo

To my daughter, and forever baby girl (now a grown adult), Aubrey. You are the origin and heart of why I do this radical work in sex ed. I am so inspired by you. Proud of you. And thankful for the journey of growing with you. I love you, BBG.

To my teen son, Tyson. Your curiosity, creativity, and playful spirit inspire me and have informed so many aspects of this work in more ways than I can express. Thank you for always being you; it's absolutely your most powerful gift and superpower. I love you, Balito.

To my tween bonus son, Owen. I am so grateful for our relationship, for our laughs, and for the many lessons your caring heart has taught me about love. I'm honored and committed to being one of your trusted adults and cheerleaders along your growing up journey. I love you, Owie.

To my parents, Mini and Manny. Thank you for always supporting me, no matter what. I don't take for granted your hard work, perseverance, and loving efforts that have made it possible for me to live out my dreams and purpose in this lifetime. I love you, Mom and Dad.

To my small and mighty team at Sex Positive Families: Caitlin Long and Ashley Gutierrez.

Caitlin, you have taught me SO much about the power of collaboration and community. Getting to cocreate and cofacilitate workshop experiences with you has been a dream! I'm excited for all we have ahead, and I cannot wait until Z is old enough to join us for a GIY session!

To my virtual assistant, Ashley. You've been a consistent presence that has formed the backbone of what's been possible within this work as it has evolved over the years. I'm grateful to be parenting in a sex positive way alongside you in this wild world! Thank you for being so patient with me and unwavering in your support of this mission.

To my authenticity reader, Leo C. Finley. I'm so grateful for our connection and the timing that allowed us to collaborate on this project. Your expertise as an educator, curriculum designer, and fierce advocate for queer youth and adults has lovingly sharpened the content within this book. I greatly appreciate your detailed, thoughtful review and feedback that have made this an affirming resource for trans, nonbinary, and gender-diverse young people.

To the entire Quirk Books team, especially my editor, Alex Arnold. Thank you for reaching out to me about this project, being patient with my anxious thoughts entering the world of traditional publishing, and challenging me to be even more creative and brave throughout the writing process. Thank you, Brianna Gilmartin, for your beautiful illustration work that brings a warm smile, and affirming life, to this content.

To my friend and mentor, Cory Silverberg. Thank you for being an unapologetic role model of liberatory, radical, youth-centered, fun puberty and sex education. Your gentle, honest, and encouraging nudges and words of wisdom over the years have been deeply felt and appreciated. They've helped me show up more bravely.

To my contract attorney, Brooks. Thank you for being a patient support to help me understand all the legal language, advocate for myself, and ultimately feel more confident in saying yes to this collaborative project.

To the ever-growing Sex Positive Families and Growing Into You!™ communities of tweens, teens, and trusted adults from around the world who have joined us over the years for our workshops, courses, newsletters, and social media content, and to the youth whose voices were included in this book. Thank you for trusting me and my team with your curiosities, a-ha moments, your families, and your healing journeys. It has been such an honor to share spaces with so many fellow cycle breakers. One day I hope there'll be a world where shame-free conversations and education about puberty, changing bodies, and sexual health are standard and no longer taboo. Until then, we're excited to continue to offer engaging, brave spaces for learning and growing together.

And finally, to Stacy Pearson, who sent me an email in 2018 asking if I'd be willing to provide puberty education to a Girl Scout troop in Austin, Texas. You asked for a workshop that would help "parents and daughters feel comfortable talking about puberty together." From this moment, Growing Into You!™ was born. I'm so grateful.

David Borgenicht Chairman and Founder
Jhanteigh Kupihea President and Publisher
Nicole De Jackmo EVP, Deputy Publisher
Andie Reid Creative Director
Jane Morley Managing Editor
Mandy Sampson Production Director
Shaquona Crews Principal, Contracts and Rights
Katherine McGuire Assistant Director of Subsidiary Rights

CREATIVE

Alex Arnold Editorial Director, Children's
Jess Zimmerman Editor
Rebecca Gyllenhaal Associate Editor
Jessica Yang Assistant Editor

Elissa Flanigan Senior Designer
Paige Graff Junior Designer
Kassie Andreadis Managing Editorial Assistant

SALES, MARKETING, AND PUBLICITY

Kate Brown Senior Sales Manager
Christina Tatulli Digital Marketing Manager
Ivy Weir Senior Publicity and Marketing Manager
Gaby Iori Publicist and Marketing Coordinator

Kim Ismael Digital Marketing Design Associate
Scott MacLean Publicity and Marketing Assistant
Jesse Mendez Sales Assistant

OPERATIONS

Kaitlyn Buszkiewic Finance Manager
Caprianna Anderson Business Associate
Robin Wright Production and Sales Assistant